Unleashing Your Authentic Power

Unleashing Your Authentic Power

Resistance-Free Living

Jim Britt

Health Communications, Inc.
Deerfield Beach, Florida

www.hci-online.com

Cataloging-in-Publication Data is on file
with The Library of Congress.

Publisher: Health Communications, Inc.
          3201 S.W. 15th Street
          Deerfield Beach, Florida 33442-8190

Cover design by Read Johns
Inside book design by Lawna Patterson Oldfield

*Dedicated to
all those who seek to know
themselves and walk the
path with heart.*

Contents

Introduction

Happiness! It's the most sought-after commodity in the world. Everyone is looking for it—from a princess trying to find a second chance at real love, to a celebrity on drugs trying to escape personal pain. People try to find it through their families and significant relationships, their careers, their religious or spiritual affiliations, sex, vacations, hobbies, cars, money and addictions. The list goes on and on.

What seems to get in the way of consistently experiencing happiness is our dramas in life. Relationship dramas. Work dramas. Health dramas. Money dramas. Family dramas. Spiritual dramas. We all have them ... from the president of the United States to the abuse victim to the single mom on welfare sitting home watching TV. The dramas are all around us. They're all we see in the news, on the talk shows, in the newspapers and magazines, in the movies, in our lives, in our friends' lives, etc. Yet, everyone from the president to the single mom on welfare is trying to figure out the same thing —how to let go and move past their dramas and how to find true "happiness."

How do we achieve REAL happiness? How do we break free of our dramas successfully? How can we let go of the emotions and pain from the past, the fear of the future, and the anxieties of daily life that are always a part of our dramas?

Recall a time in your own life when you felt worried about money, anxious about success, depressed, over-whelmed by a relationship or family problem, or by not having enough time or feeling out of control. How did that make you feel? Did it negatively affect you? How about negative feelings associated with experiences from your past? Are they hurting you in the present?

We are constantly pulled in two directions at the same time. Our desire for success and happiness inspires us to move forward, and at the same time the feelings that control our negative emotions and nonproductive behaviors hold us back. It's like driving a car with one foot on the gas and the other on the brake, wondering why we're not getting any-where! Sound familiar?

In an attempt to avoid these feelings or push them away, we have programmed our minds, made lists, learned while we slept, followed a guru, thought positively, attended recov-ery support groups, pulled our own strings, walked on fire, and more, looking for the answers. But the startling truth is, after all this, most are still searching. Why? It is the lack of a clear understanding of the part these feelings play in our lives: they literally have total control over us.

Self-improvement is not what we need. We've all had enough self-improvement to last a lifetime. What we need is waking up! Waking up to the fact that the feelings, the underlying blocks locked away in our subconscious programs, are what restrict us from living at our full potential.

It is a well-known fact that our thoughts determine our direction in life, while it is a little-known fact that the feelings we hold inside attract our circumstances. Feelings become like a magnet pulling back to us what we project from inside. The fact is our feelings run our lives. They literally block our chances at success, happiness and self-love. We've become so accustomed to our feelings that we don't even see that we are hanging on to them. Instead we feel that they are hanging on to us!

We create an exciting new vision of something we want. Then, like a thief in the night, these deeply buried feelings hidden away in our subconscious programming sneak in and take over. They push us around, offering confusing, conflicting messages, dictating what we can and cannot do. People are wandering around on automatic pilot, and their plane isn't going where they want it to go! This book will show you how to turn off the autopilot, let go, break free of your dramas and go in the direction you want to go.

The key to having all we want in life is to learn to let go

of the negative feelings held inside: not only those associated with old hurts, past mistakes and failures hidden away in our subconscious, but those we encounter as part of our daily life as well.

When you learn to let go of the emotional waste, you'll begin to enjoy abundance in every area of your life. Your financial status, health, relationships, family and personal happiness will become more than you ever thought they could be.

You'll discover in the following pages how to use your authentic power of love to attract what you want in life. You'll learn how to let go of the fears and emotions that cause your unhappiness. You'll find methods to deactivate your internal failure mechanism before it's engaged. You'll learn to forgive the past and yourself and break free from the chain of pain and leave in its place the chain of love. You'll truly know how to let go and move past your dramas, and live a life filled with joy.

There's no need for us to seek to acquire power. We already have it. Authentic power is intimately a part of us. We were born with it! We use it every day. The real problem is that we don't fully understand it and therefore don't fully utilize it.

Day by day as you begin to understand and use the processes presented herein, you will gain momentum. Your life plans will crystallize. You will gain a greater understanding of that which you truly are, the power you possess and how life really works. You'll suddenly see that the world you live in can become much more than a pile of dirt with some rocks and trees. It can become a beautiful, living thing. Once you reclaim your authentic power, you'll discover that the world is made up of the beating hearts of all humanity. The world you'll see is a thing of life, beauty and love.

1

Unhappiness Is a Learned Behavior

*Happiness
only exists when
we see that
unhappiness
is not connected
to the event itself
but rather to how
we perceive
the event*

Imagine walking into a room where groups of people are seated at a table where a delicious-looking meal is set before them. The table is filled with every sort of food you can imagine. It's a mouthwatering display of food, all perfectly prepared. It's all right in front of their noses and easily within their reach.

You notice that none of the people are eating. They haven't even taken a single bite. Their plates are empty. It appears they have been seated there for a very long time—so long that they appear to be starving to death.

They are starving not because they cannot eat the wonderful food before them, nor because eating it is forbidden or harmful. They aren't eating because they don't realize that food is what they need. They don't know that those very sharp pains in their stomachs are caused by hunger. They don't see that all they need to do to stop their suffering is eat the food that's right in front of them.

This is an example of our basic human suffering. Most of us sense that there is something wrong, that something is inherently missing in our lives, but we haven't a clue what the problem is or what we should do about it. We may see faintly that what we need is somehow very close to us, but we don't connect it to the sharp pain inside us. Even with time, as the pain becomes more severe, we can't see what we need.

We all long for something. We feel the pain. We suffer daily not knowing that everything we need to eliminate our suffering is right before us.

All the pain and suffering we experience is of our own making. It develops out of our own hearts and minds. It comes out of our own confusion. In addition, if we don't begin to see where the problems originate or what they really are, we will only increase their strength. Because it's all we know, we will teach our children the same confusion. And it will continue generation after generation, doing more of the same to ourselves and those around us. We—you and I—are the pivotal generation. For things to change in our lives, our children's lives and in the world, we must make a change. The time is NOW!

We all want to be free of our problems, but here's the bottom line. No person's life ever is, was or will be free from difficulty. All I'm offering is possibly a new way of observing the true nature of our problems, what they are and where they originated. It's not a "sit back and let it happen" philosophy. It's simply about getting to the basics. It's about getting to the root cause of our pain, and then acting on it from that point of view.

I once heard a story about a man who went to a spiritual master hoping to rid himself of his problems. He explained for hours the long list of problems he faced. He explained that even though his children were good, sometimes they just didn't respect him enough. He explained that even though he dearly loved his wife, she nagged too much. He explained that sales in his business were declining and he had barely enough money to pay his bills. The list of problems went on and on.

The master sat in silence listening to every word the man had to say. Finally the man wound down and waited for the master's response, for the master to give him the secret to handling all his problems.

When the all-knowing master finally responded he said, "I can't help you."

"What do you mean you can't help me?" the man cried.

The master said, "Well, we each have fifty-one problems, and there's nothing I or anyone else can do about it. If you work really hard on one of them, you just might fix it, but as soon as you do there'll be another to take its place. For example, you are going to die some day, and so are your wife and children. Now that's a problem, and there's absolutely nothing you or I or anyone else can do about it."

The man became very angry and shouted, "I thought you were a great master. I thought you could help solve my problems! What good are your teachings anyway?"

"Well," the master said, "maybe I can help you with your fifty-second problem, your greatest problem of all."

"My fifty-second problem!" the man shouted. "What's my fifty-second problem?"

"Your fifty-second problem," the master said, "is you want to not have any problems."

We all believe that we have to resolve each of our problems in a way that completely eliminates them, or we want to deny their reality altogether. However, in doing so, what we are really trying to do is to make reality into something other than what's really happening.

Here's the point. Life involves having problems and dealing with them. That's why we're here in the first place. Name one person who doesn't have problems and I'll show you someone without a pulse. In fact, if you're alive and you don't have problems, then you've got real problems!

Here's a good starting point. Problems are a fact of human life. Weeds will grow, even if we hate them and wish them gone. Why? That's the nature of weeds. They will grow without our planting them. Flowers, on the other hand, will grow, wither and die, even though we love them and want them to remain.

How do you feel about this reality? Maybe we should all just pretend there are no weeds. Maybe we should all just pretend that all we love is not going to eventually die. Maybe we should just pretend there are no problems and see what happens. We've all become pretty good at that one. All we need to do is just look around. Our whole planet is in denial. That's why we have so many problems.

It's important to realize that all our dissatisfactions originate within us. They arise out of our ignorance, or our being blind to reality, or our desire for reality to be something other than what it is. It is this wanting reality to be something other than what it is that dissatisfies us in the first place.

Life is a journey. The journey should be one of getting to know our true selves once again, a journey into nearness and self-intimacy. Our real journey is to awaken to the here and now, to be fully alive and fully present in this moment, in this reality. After all, this moment is all there is anyway. Why would we want to be anywhere else?

We must come to three realizations in order to find happiness. First, we must realize that life is fleeting. It's passing us by, moment to moment. Next, we must realize that we are already complete, whole and worthy of happiness. Last, we must see that we are our own refuge, our own sanctuary and our own salvation. We need nothing from the outside to make us more, or to provide us with happiness.

We've Become Attached to Our Pain

As we've discussed, life involves pain and unhappiness. Wouldn't you agree? We could define pain as anything from displeasure or dissatisfaction to failure, a relationship breakup, lack of money, or the death of a loved one.

Most of us continue to choose our old way, the way that causes us pain or unhappiness, because we're good at doing it. We retreat to the familiar. It's what we know, and it's who we believe we are. It feels safe and comfortable. We know exactly how to do it. After all, we've been doing it all our lives. The reason we continue with our old methods is because there's no risk. Before most of us would risk moving out of our comfort zone, things would have to get pretty stressful. In other words, we'd have to become pretty miserable before we'd let go of our ideas about how we think life should be. We'd have to let go of our belief about what really constitutes happiness.

The only reason we have unhappiness is because we continue to hang on to what we believe happiness should be. We refuse to let go of our old belief systems, our feelings and our old habit patterns.

Our pain and unhappiness are caused by our unwillingness to accept what is, right now, and to let go of the past and our expectations of the future. We discover our willingness to let go of our old ways only when the pain becomes more than we can handle.

There are basically five reasons for our unhappiness:

1. Not getting what we want in life.
2. Getting what we want but not being satisfied with it.
3. Suffering the absence of something or someone we love.
4. Enduring the presence of something or someone we do not want in our lives.
5. Our greatest concern: living in the past or in the future; not being here now.

How we respond to the above leads us either toward or further away from happiness. Throughout this book, you'll be encouraged to observe yourself to discover why you do what you do, and why you continue to make the choices you make. You'll be encouraged to see whether your thoughts, beliefs, feelings, language, behaviors and perceptions cause you to experience happiness or move you away from it.

Let's begin by exploring our thoughts, beliefs, feelings, language and behaviors. Observing these areas allows us an opportunity to see ourselves a little more clearly. We'll begin to see how we approach life, how we think, how powerful our words are, how we choose our values, why we embrace certain behaviors and how our beliefs and feelings affect our lives.

You shouldn't concern yourself about what you are doing right or wrong, because neither will apply. It's not my objective to persuade you to do anything about how you think, believe, feel, speak or behave. However, I would like for you to have an open mind, explore the whole process and see how these things are affecting your life. As the process unfolds, I'd like you to focus upon you and not on the content of your life. What you think, believe, feel, speak or your behaviors will not be the point. Why you do it will be the point.

You may, for example, hold a belief that life is difficult. That's a very simple statement, one that is heard often. Here's what I want to encourage you to do. I want you to observe yourself, and to explore how you came to believe that life is difficult. Who taught you to believe that? What sequence of events supported that belief? More importantly, how has having that belief affected your life? Does it add to your happiness? Does it help to ease your pain? Or does it cause you to suffer more?

What would happen to your life if you suddenly challenged that belief? How would your life be different? That's the real issue. My purpose is to get you to ask yourself why you have certain beliefs, and for you to ask yourself, "What if it's not true?" I want you to ask yourself, "Is this belief really necessary? Or for that matter, is any belief necessary?" I just want to encourage you to back off and observe how you are living your life. That's the real purpose of this book.

This book isn't about motivation. We've had enough motivation to last a lifetime. Motivation is self-addition. What we need is self-correction. We need awakening! We need to discover what de-motivates us, not how to get re-motivated every time we feel down or things aren't going our way. What we truly need to discover is what has turned us off. Getting turned on is easy. We can do that at the drop of a hat. Staying turned on is the problem that faces us every waking moment. Finding out what keeps turning us off is the key to happiness. Only when we can discover what's holding us back and causing us to suffer will we find happiness.

Beliefs, Our Only Obstacle

We're going to first explore our beliefs, then how our thinking supports our beliefs, how our beliefs were created, and how our feelings act as magnets that attract our life circumstances, which in turn influence our thoughts and beliefs once again.

- Thoughts choose our direction and influence our behavior
- Behaviors create experiences
- Experiences create feelings
- Feelings attract circumstances
- Circumstances form beliefs
- Beliefs motivate language and behavior
- Language and behaviors influence our thoughts once again

A mutually supporting cycle is created.

So what is a belief anyway? The definition of *belief* is "something accepted as real or true." Does this then make all beliefs true? No. To define the word further we should say, "A belief is something that we decide is true." It may not be at all. For example, you may believe that life is tough, and I might believe that life is a joyful experience. Someone else might believe that life is good only under certain circumstances. So which is true? All three? None of them? What it really depends upon is your view of life. A belief is something that we decide should be true, based upon our perceptions of life.

A belief is simply a belief, nothing more, nothing less. It is our opinion of how we think things should be. Whatever our belief may be, it has total control over our life. Our life today is a reflection of the way we believed it would be in the past. Restated, our life today results from our past beliefs. Attempting to change a belief and replace it with a new one can be like hitting your head against a brick wall. However, this does not have to be true when you learn how to approach it and what originally created the belief. The brick wall can come down, but not by continually hitting it with our heads (which we tend to do repeatedly). Banging our head against it will only cause us more pain, as most of us have already discovered. What we have not discovered is how to stop. Is there a simpler, less painful way? We must first see the brick wall before we can stop hitting it.

We've all heard the expression "Seeing is believing." What we need to realize, however, is that believing is not "true seeing" or "seeing truth." In fact, they are quite the opposite. We should know that our belief of how something should be is nothing more than a partially informed guess about reality. On the other hand, a direct experience is the direct perception of reality itself.

As an example, let us say I hold in front of you two closed fists. I tell you that one holds a hundred-dollar bill, and if you guess the correct hand, the money is yours. Now, I may be lying or I may be telling the truth. Only I know the truth. Only I can see reality. Either way you do not really know as long as I keep my hand closed. The most you can do is to speculate or believe that I might have the money in one hand or the other.

As I open my hands, the usefulness of your belief completely vanishes, does it not? Why is this so? Because now you know of what reality consists. You now know the truth.

So it is with any question, situation or problem you may face. Your belief may serve as a useful tool in the absence of actual experience, but once you see reality, belief becomes unnecessary. The fact is that our beliefs often stand in the way of our actually seeing reality.

I was speaking before a Christian church a few years ago. About five minutes into my talk a woman up close to the front suddenly blurted out, "Excuse me, young man, but do you believe in God?" I answered, "No, I don't believe in God." Looking very startled when she heard my answer, she again asked, "You don't believe in God?" My answer again was, "No, I don't believe in God." At this point there were about four hundred very startled people looking at me. The woman then asked, "How could you have the nerve to speak before our congregation and not believe in God?" My response was, "I don't believe in God, I know God." With a big sigh of relief and a big smile she said, "Oh wow, that's wonderful!"

The first step in changing a belief is to know that we cannot rely on it if we wish to see truth or reality. We can only rely on actual perception or direct experience.

You don't have to go to someone—a teacher, master, priest, your parents, a shaman or any other authority—in order to change a belief and see reality. Truth comes from direct experience. To see is to know.

Some spend their lives trying to find happiness by saying they get their answers by communicating with life-forms on other planets. We could even believe that there are beings on other planets that hold the answers to our happiness. My question is, even if life does exist on other planets—and no one really knows for sure—what do they know about finding happiness on *this* planet, where we already know life exists? Life is about here and now. Happiness is about here and now. Happiness is about seeing life the way it is versus the way we wish it would be. Happiness comes from seeing truth.

Our attempt to avoid seeing our experience for what it is in order to avoid pain is what is causing our pain in the first place.

Let us say, for example, that you previously had a painful relationship. You now feel that you are ready for a new one. You, of course, do not want to get hurt again, so you are going to proceed into your new relationship with caution. You are going to proceed with your heart closed in order to be protected until you know for sure that this person is the right one. Then you will open your heart.

Approaching a new relationship with a closed heart is avoiding reality, because with a closed heart you will be unable to see the truth. We want to overlook truth in order to avoid the pain, not knowing that what we are really attracting is more pain. In our desperate attempt to avoid pain, we will very likely repeat the same mistake. The cycle will continue until we let go of our fears and approach the new relationship with an open heart where we can see truth.

How do we create our beliefs? One way is through repetition. If we see, hear, think and experience something often enough, or long enough, it can become a belief. For example, if as children we observed our parents fighting all the time, we might grow up believing that is the way all relationships function. Because of this belief, we repeat the same pattern in our own relationships. We may have grown up with a dominating father and a submissive mother. Usually in this case, later in life, a child takes on one of those traits in their relationship. It might even be a reversed role. The son observes the dominating father and becomes a submissive adult.

A child may repeatedly hear statements from his or her parents such as, "You'll never amount to anything," or "We're poor, and when you grow up you'll be the same because you're just like your father." This sort of upbringing may cause the child to grow up with a lot of self-doubt and to feel unworthy about having money.

The opposite may also happen. A person could grow up in a wealthy family and observe what having money and using it correctly can do to people. The child decides that money is bad and consequently struggles with money as an adult.

Parents may yell frequently at their child. As the child grows older this could result in his holding on to a lot of built-up anger. Since the child is afraid of expressing himself, he holds it all inside. As this happens increasingly and over time, it becomes a belief that he should not express himself, or it may become a belief that when he does express himself, it should be with much force.

As we grow up, and even later in life, it is as if we are walking around with an invisible computer keyboard strapped to us. The only problem is that it's turned outward, ready and waiting for anyone and everyone to give us input on how we should or should not live our lives. In doing so they then metaphorically press "Enter."

"I told you not to do that!" Enter. "When will you ever learn?" Enter. "Why don't you ever listen?" Enter. "I'll give you something to cry about!" Enter. "You should be ashamed of yourself." Enter. "Don't touch that, you'll go blind!" Enter. "Just once, why don't you do something right?" Enter. "You little brat, it's all your fault!" Enter. "Money doesn't grow on trees." Enter. And on and on.

Somewhere along the way, we developed a belief that says, "There must be something wrong with me." What else could we think? *There's something wrong with me, otherwise I would be happy, and I wouldn't have so much pain in my life. If something were not wrong with me, my life would be working.*

A parent shared a story with me that her ten-year-old son wrote as a school report. The story was about the Bengal tiger. The story started with a beautiful description of how and where Bengal tigers live. Then it suddenly changed to something like, "I hate my life. My parents don't even love me. They got divorced because of me. They fight all the time and get really angry with each other. When they fight they sometimes get mad at me and it makes me sad. It's all because of me. It's all my fault that my parents aren't together anymore."

Well-meaning parents often unknowingly taught us certain behaviors. There is no one to blame for how we turned out. Our parents did their best based upon what they believed. We adopted certain beliefs and behaviors into our lives that we felt we needed in order to just survive. The same well-meaning parents then taught us to hate those behavioral traits and to see them as bad.

As children, we may have been told repeatedly not to speak unless spoken to, or that kids should be seen and not heard. Because of this repeated input, we now have a tremendous fear of speaking in front of others. When we bring our report card home reflecting this problem, our parents now tell us to have courage, to stand up and be heard!

Here is the trap that was created. "I believe I must be this way in order to survive" (the result of past programming). Moreover, "I hate myself for feeling the way I do." The result is this:

Self-judgment =
I have to be this way in order to survive.
I have to be this way in order to survive =
Self-judgment.

SURVIVAL

SELF-JUDGMENT

We have been taught to believe this way. Why do you suppose we had to be *taught* to believe this way? Because it is not true, that's why. It isn't reality. If we could just observe our lives for a moment with an unconditioned mind, we would see that not only is this not true, but it is absolutely ridiculous!

To top it off, we then begin to create a self-judgment report card for ourselves. We look at what we have accomplished compared to everyone else. We look at the things we own compared to everyone else. We look at who we think we've become compared to everyone else.

We then create our report card.

What we've accomplished,
 compared to our neighbor . . . . .C-
What we own, compared to our coworkers . . . . . .B+

Who we've become, compared to others

with the same education . . . . .D

Then the silent whispers kick in, supporting the beliefs we hold about ourselves. *"I shouldn't feel this way." "Won't I ever learn? I should have known better." "That was really a dumb thing to do! I can't believe I did it again."*

There you have it, our very own self-judgment accounting system. We are always clinging to what should have been, or what we should have done or the way we think things should be.

We think that our beliefs and ideas, our accounting system, can be relied upon to give us satisfaction. But if we examine the effect it is having on us, we'll see that at best it only brings temporary satisfaction. In fact, our self-accounting system is actually our primary source of anxiety and fear, because it always places doubt in our minds.

Doubt is the flip side of belief. As soon as we look at belief, doubt arises with it. The two are inseparable. The moment we hold some false idea about ourselves rather than relying on a direct perception of what's really happening, we inevitably give rise to anxiety or fear. We create our own suffering through the repetition of our confusion. Our life becomes like driving our car with a flat tire. It moves along, but the ride is a little rough and slow. We're always thinking that something is wrong, but we're not exactly sure what's causing the bumping.

The same goes with our lives. We feel there's something out there we've got to get, and there are things out there we've got to keep away from in order to be happy. This becomes a mutually self-supporting system for our own out-dated beliefs and false perceptions. It keeps them alive and well, and the bumping continues.

The wanting and craving for something outside us becomes the trap. Our job is seeing what doesn't make sense when things are not working. In other words, seeing the truth. Our confusion and head-bashing against that brick wall come from our own illusionary belief that we are separate from what's really going on. We believe that something or someone out there is doing it to us.

The Power of Emotional Impact

The second way our beliefs are created is through emotional impact.

Let's say, for example, that as a four-year-old child you loved to pick flowers and give them to your mother. While picking flowers from your neighbor's yard one day, not aware that you were doing anything wrong, the neighbor, a very tall and big man, confronted you. "You little brat, you're the one who's been picking my flowers! Wait till I get my hands on you! You're going to be in a lot of trouble!"

With this sort of emotional impact as a child, you could grow up believing "Tall people are mean"; "You can't trust tall people"; or "I'm afraid of tall people, they'll hurt you." As an adult, it may show up as a person who just can't seem to get along with tall men, and we don't even know why.

Another example might be in relationships. Like so many people today, we may have grown up in a broken home. Maybe we've heard repeatedly that relationships are hard to keep together, and over 50 percent end in divorce. Maybe we've grown up with divorced parents and believe it to be true in all relationships.

I remember a young woman in one of my classes. We were discussing relationships and marriage when the woman spoke up and said that even though she would love to have a loving marriage, she would never get married. With some further discussion and questioning, she said that her parents were the reason. She said that she would never forget when she was eleven years old that her parents came in and told her they were getting a divorce. She said that at that very moment she decided that she was never going to get married. She developed a belief, due to the severe emotional impact she had experienced, that marriage would end in pain, a pain that she didn't want to experience again. Because of our false beliefs, we can no longer see reality; we are blinded by our perceptions of what we believe to be truth. Stop for a moment, sit back, relax and observe your own beliefs.

What do you believe about relationships? How's that belief working for you? What are your money beliefs? What have you heard about money? "Money doesn't grow on trees. There's not enough money to go around. You can't be spiritual and have money. Money is the root of all evil." What do you believe about money? How's that belief working for you?

I'd like to encourage you to examine your beliefs about relationships, money, career, family, health, and spirituality, and how those beliefs are working for you. Stop and reflect for a moment. *How did this particular belief originate? Who says it's true?*

Are all relationships difficult? No!

Do all relationships end in divorce? No!

Are all teenagers difficult to raise? No!

Does everyone live with lack? No!

Remember that a belief is what we decide is true, yet it may not be true at all.

Thoughts Choose Your Direction

The next thing to discuss is our thoughts. As human beings we think altogether too much, and about altogether too many things. Within a single moment our mind can contemplate a vast number of unrelated concepts and half-formed ideas—more thoughts than could be found on the pages of a dictionary. One second we're looking out over a beautiful meadow and the mountains in the distance. The next thing we know we're suffering with anxiety over problems in our business. Then a split second later our thoughts are at home with the family. We jump around haphazardly from one thought to another, totally unguided and unguarded. We buy in to whatever happens to be presented across our mental movie screen and determine that it must be real or true.

Because the human is a multilevel machine, it is good to know that some of our thoughts are in the development stage, while others are on their way to completion. In other words, thoughts proceed in a continuing series. For example, while you are engaged in some activity, you may also be eating, driving your car or walking. You may also be thinking about that new outfit you are going to buy and that vacation you want to take. In other words, you are thinking on several levels.

Your brain proceeds to bring your desires into fruition by seeking out your options—where to go to purchase that new outfit, where to go on your vacation, and so on. This is the multidimensional aspect of the human mind and its activity. We can do one thing and be thinking about several other things at the same time. We could have hundreds of activities going on at the same time.

The law of attraction never stops, and without realizing it, we are planting a seed with each thought. We start the thought process moving in one direction, stop it, start it again in another direction, recall it, send it off again—and we do it hundreds of times every hour. We have developed habits of totally and absolutely undisciplined thinking.

We are thinking about some project we are working on at the office, then suddenly a thought about a personal issue pops into our mind. Without stopping to complete the first thought, we are now thinking about something else. What we've done in this case is sent a half-finished message off to the universe for answers. What do you think we'll receive back? Right! A half-finished answer. What kind of harvest should we expect from our planting?

One moment we feel happy and entertain happy thoughts, and then we get a telephone call that didn't go the way we wanted, and now we feel unhappy and entertain unhappy thoughts.

A friend pays us a compliment, "That is a beautiful outfit you are wearing," and we feel great. An acquaintance criticizes us, "That outfit, while it is very nice, makes you look too tall," and we now feel resentful. Often, where any discipline exists, it is aimed at nonresourceful thinking such as worry, anxiety, fear and doubt. What we're really attempting to avoid is the feelings that keep our beliefs alive, which in turn influence our thoughts and behaviors.

We always seem to be waiting for input from the outside to determine which thoughts we will reject and which we will accept. We become victims of other people's thoughts and belief systems. Our life becomes a never-ending chain of circumstances over which we feel we have no control.

There's a story about a bricklayer working three stories up on a scaffold. When he finished the job he had a scaffold full of bricks left over. He didn't want to throw them down and break them, so he tied a rope to a large bucket and ran the rope over a pulley. He filled the bucket with bricks and climbed to the ground. He then grabbed the rope and pulled, allowing the bucket full of bricks to swing out so he could lower them to the ground. To his surprise, the bucket of bricks was heavier than he was, and down they came. Startled, he hung on to the rope, and up he went. He and the bricks collided halfway, and he got banged up. When he hit the top, his fingers became caught in the pulley. At the same time, the bucket of bricks hit the ground, spilling some.

He's now heavier than the bucket of bricks. Still holding on to the rope, he goes down and the bricks come up. Again they meet in the middle, and again he gets banged around. He finally hits the ground and lets go of the rope. Now, the bucket of bricks weighs more than the rope, so the bucket of bricks hurtles down, hitting him on the head.

That is called a chain of circumstances. He got the job done, but he sure got beat up in the process, wouldn't you agree? Do you think he might want to consider a different approach next time?

Without even stopping to consider the potential outcome, many of us approach our daily challenges in much the same way.

A Higher Intelligence on Our Side

We have a vast intelligence at work for us. Our conscious mind is like a sensory organ that keeps this intelligence informed about the circumstances in any given situation. Whatever conclusions we reach on a conscious level are forwarded to this higher intelligence and then returned to us in physical reality. That's simply the law of nature.

When our thoughts become conclusive and are backed up by emotions and feelings and then turned into reality, we can't stop the process. It is automatic. We can only control our thinking and the feelings supporting our beliefs, which in turn influence our thoughts. First, all of our thoughts are not turned into physical reality, if they are not convictions of the heart. In other words, if they are just passing thoughts, they are thoughts to which we have no emotional attachment. Such thoughts are not passed on to the higher intelligence. Second, we sometimes change our thoughts, thereby canceling out the original ones.

This may be difficult to comprehend, but every thought backed up with a conviction is manifested instantaneously. Thoughts that don't manifest instantaneously flounder because we simply lose our conviction toward that thought or goal. Let's say that we have a goal to earn a certain amount of money within a given time frame. Our mind goes to work. It offers conflicting thoughts. It tells us why we don't deserve it, or how hard it will be, etc. This, in turn, creates a whole new goal or direction. These opposing thoughts are triggered by our belief systems. Our beliefs are kept alive by suppressed energy patterns known as feelings, which are the result of some past experience we haven't yet resolved.

I remember the first goal I ever set. It was to earn $10,000 in one month. The problem was that at that time the most I had ever earned in one month was about $350. This was a far cry from $10,000, but I was determined. Around the first of each month I would tell everybody my goal. About the tenth of the month the self-talk started. "You've never earned that much before. You don't have an education; you're a high school dropout. You don't deserve that much money." Around the fifteenth of the month, I would lower my goal to $5,000. About the twentieth I would drop it again. Then I would disappear for the rest of the month because I felt so bad about not having accomplished what I had bragged about. I was beginning to believe my own self-talk.

At the end of each month, my earnings would end up at about $350. Why? That's where I saw my value. That was my degree of clarity toward my objective. It took me years of continued effort to finally achieve that goal. At the time, I didn't understand how simple it was to change my outdated belief.

So, if all of our convictions are manifested instantaneously, why does it seem to take so long to create the results we desire? The speed of the results is totally based on our clarity of thought—without interference. Our strongest convictions determine our results.

The Magnet That Attracts Circumstances

Faith is our most important tool in molding and determining outcomes. Faith is simply the tool that gives conviction to our visions. Faith impresses the thought upon the higher intelligence as a conviction . . . and convictions become reality.

If we hold a clear conviction that we'll produce a certain outcome, and if there is no conflicting belief that produces a conflicting conviction, then the conviction will become a reality. If the higher intelligence receives the convictions that we have perfect health, a fulfilling career, a loving relationship or any other desire, we will manifest those things in our lives.

Let me offer a more detailed example. Suppose you set out to open your own business. You certainly thought it would be a super success, otherwise you wouldn't have started it in the first place.

Suppose you have purchased an inventory of merchandise to stock your shelves. The doors are open and you offer it for sale, but no one wants to buy it. No one even comes into your store. Your immediate feeling is that you've made a serious mistake. This thought is closely followed by another thought, that you are going to lose a sizable amount of money. Before long, if you don't create a new vision of success, you'll begin to visualize or become convinced that your business is a failure. You may even begin to see yourself as bankrupt, with no hope at all, a victim of cruel fate.

Think about it. What would be your reaction? What would be your conviction, success or failure? Which would you honor the most, your vision of a successful business or your problems at hand? Chances are that probably a large part of your attention might be focused upon failure. As long as a conviction of failure predominates in your mind, you will eventually fail, or you will only be a success to the degree that you are convinced of your success. A feeling of either success or failure will back every action you take. That feeling becomes like a magnet to attract the circumstances necessary to fulfill your conviction. That is one of the reasons some businesses are more successful than others. It may not be the only reason, but it's certainly at the top of the list. You've got to think and feel successful in order to become so. It's impossible to be a success in any endeavor while thinking and feeling failure. In fact if you think success and feel failure, guess what? Failure. It works the same whether it's in your business, relationship, family, career or health. Whatever you give attention to grows.

Remember the story I told earlier about my goal to earn $10,000 in one month? That's exactly what was happening to me. I was thinking success but feeling failure. Until I aligned the two, nothing happened.

I will repeat this again: The tools that we must use to prevent such circumstances from entering our lives are vision and faith. We must have a clear vision of the success of our objective, and we must trust the process.

In order to have faith, we must learn to let go of the non-resourceful feelings that keep our nonfaith feelings and beliefs alive. In the preceding example, the critical point at which faith and letting go must be exercised is the point at which it becomes apparent there are no buyers for the merchandise you have in inventory.

At this point refusing to accept your circumstances as a mistake or as an indicator of forthcoming failure is the key. The solution is not to think positive or affirm the problem away, but to have faith that everything is unfolding perfectly. When we stay focused on the problem, we see no way out. When we let go of our fears, we allow new solutions to open up to us. This doesn't mean that we don't take action to change. All it means is that we're taking action from a more solution-oriented place. We need to trust and to have faith that there is something greater at work directing us along the correct path.

It's also important to know that it is not up to us to determine the ways and means and the correct sequence of events by which we will attain success. However, it is up to us to let go of our fears, and to have faith and conviction that everything is unfolding perfectly. So, instead of always worrying about tomorrow, develop the understanding that there is no intelligence at all in worry. Our real problems arise not from what happens to us but rather from the worries and demands of what we think should be happening, or by what we are concerned may not happen.

Imagine taking a picture with your camera. You have it focused—perfectly framed for the perfect shot—and you snap the camera. Then right after you snap the picture you open up the camera to see if the picture came out all right. You wouldn't do that, would you? The same should apply to any vision. We create the vision of the end result we want to produce and then trust the process, whether it's a camera or a vision of our life purpose.

There are always two things at work: intention and attention. *Intention* is the focus we have toward our objective. Through having a clear intention, all the things we need to focus our *attention* on in order to accomplish our intention are brought forth. Without intention, there is nothing on which to focus our attention. How could there be? No focus, no direction. No reason to do anything.

I remember once having a very clear intention to open a combination medical/nutrition clinic. The only problem was I had no experience at either. I knew I could hire nutritionists and medical doctors, but I needed someone for a certain procedure I wanted to offer. The second person I spoke to about it referred me to a man who sold the test kits for the procedure I wanted to offer.

I met with the man and told him what I planned to do. He said with a chuckle, "Let me save you a lot of time and money. I opened a clinic in San Francisco just like what you are talking about, and it didn't work. I did a total of sixteen hundred dollars of business in the first year."

My immediate response to him was, "What does your lack of success have to do with mine?" As we talked further, he looked at me and said, "You really intend to do this, don't you?" I said, "Not only do I intend to do it, I intend to be a super success!"

He looked at me for a moment and responded, "I believe you are going to be a success. Would you like a partner?" My intention was so strong that it created a belief in him.

To make a long story short, we formed a partnership, and within two weeks we had opened our clinic. By the end of the first year we had opened four clinics that were all very successful.

A clear intention will always show you exactly what you need to devote your attention to in order to produce your desired results.

We should take to heart the old adage: "In every apparent failure lies the seed of a greater opportunity." But faith and intention are required to be open to see the opportunity. When we have faith and conviction in what we're doing, we will find a market for our goods, created perhaps in a totally different manner than originally envisioned.

I know a man who developed a product and was determined to sell it in drugstores. After several years of very limited success and eventual failure, instead of giving up he proceeded with faith and conviction that his product was going to be a massive success. A short time later he was asked to put his product on television as an infomercial. In less than three years he had made a net profit of more than $120 million. Intention is the key—intention and having faith that a higher intelligence will meet us with the correct answer on whatever level of consciousness we choose to experience. When we have intention, what we need to focus our attention upon to accomplish our objective will always appear.

The world we perceive is the world we'll create. Our world is simply a reflection of how we think, believe, feel and act, with a primary emphasis on how we feel, because feelings are the magnets that draw our circumstances to us.

The Head Initiates and Feelings Motivate

Thoughts (products of the conscious mind) choose our direction. They are the goal setters. All creation begins with an idea. An idea is simply a thought. As we think about something long enough, it will eventually become a belief. Let's say we have an idea that we are going to start a new business. Our thought process goes to work to search out all the beliefs we have that either support or discredit our initial idea. A new belief is now born as a result of collecting all the beliefs we have toward that initial idea.

Let's take a look for a moment at our feelings. Remember that our feelings are trapped experiences. Feelings create beliefs, and of course beliefs also support the feelings that motivate us into action. When we produce a result we create a whole new experience that supports our beliefs and feelings and influences our thinking (our direction chooser) once again.

Recall a time in your life when you felt worried about money, success, a relationship conflict or a family problem. How did that make you feel? Are these problems still affecting you today, even though they happened in the past? If so, that's because you are caught in a self-defeating cycle.

We all want more out of life, but our nonresourceful feelings and beliefs from the past—those that don't support how we want our life to be—are always present to create more self-imposed limitations. How do you suppose most of us handle these feelings? We don't. More times than not, they handle us! We are literally pulled in two directions at the same time. Our vision of how we want our lives to be motivates us to move forward, and our nonresourceful feelings of doubt, fear, worry and the like pull us back again.

We make an almost desperate attempt to avoid or to push these feelings away (to live a more fulfilling life). We program our minds, make lists, develop new habits, learn while we sleep, think positively, attend recovery support groups, pull our own strings, walk on fire and more—all the time looking for the answers. But the startling truth is that even after this entire series of experiences, most of us are still searching. Why? Because our feelings have total control over us. They are always lurking, trying to influence our every decision and action. They literally block our success and happiness. We create a new vision of what we want and then, like a thief in the night, our nonresourceful feelings that are hidden away step in and take over. They push us around, dictating what we can and cannot do with our lives.

So what do we do? What is the answer to handling non-supportive feelings? How do we change a belief that no longer serves us? In most cases we attempt to do so by only changing our thought process. We've been taught to believe that if we can just think positively, everything will be all right.

When we look at the deeper meaning of the word *resourceful,* it looks like this: re-source-ful—defined as "once again full of the source." The source is defined as "where all things originate." It is also defined as "love." If all things originate in the source or in love, why would we not want to live from there? How do we live from source? We simply create our vision of our desired outcome in any area of our life, and we let go of any thought, belief, feeling or behavior that doesn't support that desired outcome.

If you lack money and you are focused on "lack of money," is that moving you closer to or further away from money? Is it re-source-ful or non-re-source-ful?

If you are angry at your partner for some reason, does that anger resolve anything? Does it strengthen your relationship or weaken it? Is it re-source-ful or non-re-source-ful?

Does disciplining your child from a place of anger resolve the issue? Does it move you closer to a solution or further away?

If you are sick does focusing on your illness help to make you feel better or worse? Does it move you closer to being healthy or further away?

If you just lost your job, does being angry and resentful toward your prior boss help you to find a new job? Does it leave you open for new solutions?

The question in your mind should always be . . . is what I'm thinking, feeling, believing or the action I'm taking moving me closer to my desired results or further away? Is it re-source-ful or non-re-source-ful?

That's the main focus of this book. To get you to become more self-observant of your own actions and the results they produce.

Positive thinking to overcome self-limiting beliefs is like walking forward with a giant rubber band around your waist attached to a tree behind you. You move forward a little, but then the moment that you relax a bit, those hidden feelings pull you right back to your starting point again. Many people have become what I call "positive-thinking growth junkies." They rush from one experience to the next, looking for the hottest new technique, someone with something new to say that will enlighten them. They look for the ultimate experience that will re-create the mountaintop high once again.

Using positive thinking to overcome outdated beliefs will only create short-term patchwork solutions, and it completely misses the point of letting go.

What does positive thinking mean anyway? What is *positive?* Where does negative end and positive begin? Who says so? Positive and negative may mean different things to different people. What's positive to one may seem negative to another.

It seems that we are always beating ourselves up over being negative and seeing it as wrong, and we try too hard to be positive, seeing it as right. Of course the concept of right and wrong is another story, which we'll get into in a later chapter. The words *positive* and *negative* can be replaced with *re-source-ful* and *non-re-source-ful*. *Resourceful* and *nonresourceful* beliefs are simply those that support our vision of how we want or don't want our lives to be. If we are feeling resourceful, we are in the flow and are moving closer toward our desired outcome with every action we take. If we're feeling nonresourceful, we're out of the flow and are moving away from our desired outcome.

Michelangelo was once asked how he created such beautiful sculpture out of a piece of stone. He replied, "I simply hold a vision in my mind of what I want to create, and I chip away what doesn't support my desired outcome."

I am often asked, "What about motivation? Isn't motivation important?" Some people believe that you can't stay focused if you aren't motivated. It's an error in thinking to mistake excitement or arousal with staying focused. Motivation and emotional adventures may arouse us, but they will not enhance our sense of clarity. Motivation can exhaust our vital energy as well as our creative imagination.

We could look at motivation as the tension created when

stimulation meets resistance—stimulation created from want, which is based upon our lack of having something in the past, and resistance created from the fear of not having that which we lack.

So lack and the fear of not having create a false sense of motivation called *fear motivation,* which produces anxiety, not focus. The motivation ends when either the stimulation ends or the person wears out. With resourcefulness, on the other hand, there is no resistance. We simply create our vision of a given outcome, trust in the process, then play with whoever shows up to play, knowing that it's the right person. With resourcefulness there is no resistance, only focus and flow. If we find ourselves out of focus or not feeling right about things, it's simply a signal that there's something we need to let go of in order to move past the obstacle.

Let's say that you have a certain job to do but you find yourself continually being faced with obstacles that hold you back. If you stop and take a closer look, you may find that you are experiencing fear or some form of anxiety. By letting go of your fear and anxiety, you will find new, resourceful solutions coming to you to get the job done.

Motivation and excitement are both rooted in passing desires and instant gratification, whereas resourcefulness is rooted in source, where all things originate.

Convictions of the heart are rooted in source. When we are truly passionate and committed for the right reasons to what we want, then we are operating from source.

Do you think motivation works as a means of truly being happy? We might look around and see how many people really accomplish what they want. For those who attain any level of material success, how many are truly happy?

Affirmations: A Solution or a Problem?

Another misconception held by many is that we can change a belief through the use of affirmations. The use of affirmations to change a belief is at best a low-level activity. Affirmations are only effective in changing our minds. Beliefs can only be changed through releasing the feeling energy that keeps them alive. Beliefs are supported and maintained by suppressed feelings. Feelings are in turn created by our beliefs. A mutually dependent cycle exists. Beliefs create feelings; feelings support beliefs; beliefs create feelings; and so on.

As an example, we may experience fear when our belief about financial security is threatened, even if the belief is irrational. The fear is then suppressed and maintains the belief. Thoughts can also support our beliefs. Our beliefs can and do influence our thinking, and of course feelings influence our thinking as well. This addictive cycle will continue until it is broken by releasing the supporting feeling. Experiences = Feelings = Beliefs = Behaviors = Circumstances = Thoughts, which lead to Experiences once again. Affirming "I have no fear about not having money" while maintaining a poverty belief will not make us wealthy. It might change our thoughts temporarily, but eventually the feeling that keeps the belief alive will return. Not only that, but the affirmation could even support a poverty consciousness, especially if the feeling of frustration is present while we are speaking (affirming) the words. For example, we could affirm "I have money." This could trigger a feeling of frustration—a feeling that we are lying to ourselves—because we know full well that we don't have any money.

If we are going to use an affirmation at all, we should use one that does not confront the feeling directly. Instead, we could say something like, "Money is being irresistibly drawn to me from everywhere," or "I am at one with a tremendous amount of money right now." By doing this we are now allowing money to flow to us instead of supporting the fear of not having money. We are no longer lying to ourselves about having money, or compounding the problem.

You may have a belief that money is hard to get and doesn't flow at all in your life and that you have to go out and get it. The most resourceful approach is to create the vision in your mind and heart of how much money you want, and why you want it. Next, let go of any feeling that doesn't support that vision. Letting go requires a lot less time and certainly a lot less energy.

Let's say that you want to save $25,000 for the down payment on a new home within a certain time frame, but you've never done it before. You have a belief and a corresponding feeling of doubt about saving that amount of money in a given period of time. The key is to focus your attention on letting go of the doubt that keeps the nonsupportive belief alive, while at the same time taking action to create the money.

Here's another example of using affirmations in an ineffective way. Let's say you are affirming that you are experiencing a loving relationship, when in fact you are desperately lonely. This type of affirmation could trigger an emotional response that would accentuate your feeling of loneliness.

A man in one of my classes in Nova Scotia carried a written list of all the assets he expected in a woman. He knew exactly what he wanted: color of hair, color of eyes, height, weight, age, measurements, etc. The first thing every morning upon awakening, and the last thing before he went to bed, he would affirm, "I have a loving relationship with a woman with dark green eyes, dark hair, etc." I asked him, "How is that affirmation working for you?" He said, "Not very well." He said that he had been affirming it for over a year, twice each day, and his loneliness had actually become worse, not better. Next I asked him how he felt when he repeated his affirmation. He said, "I feel like I'm lying to myself." He said that "frustration" was what he really felt, even more so than loneliness.

Here's a question for you: Do you feel that his feeling of frustration was resourceful or nonresourceful? Will his feeling bring him closer to his desired results, or further away?

Next, I asked him how having the perfect relationship would make him feel. He said, "Wonderful."

My suggestion for him was as follows: First, throw away the list, which he did on the spot with great enthusiasm! Second, he was to get in touch with the feeling he would like to have in a personal relationship. Third, he was to observe how he felt in his current situation. And finally, he was to let go of any feeling he had that did not support his feeling of how he wanted his life to be regarding his relationships, which he did on the spot in class. Within a couple of weeks, he wrote me telling of the woman he'd met in the class, and that he was in love for the very first time in his life. I saw him almost three years later and he's still living his perfect relationship.

Thoughts plus feelings attract! Thoughts choose the direction, and our feelings attract our circumstances.

Changing Beliefs Requires Letting Go, Not Pushing Against

Our beliefs are what we are working so hard to change. Imagine that our beliefs are like a brick wall. An affirmation is like hitting our head against the wall. When we hit our head against it, it hurts! The more do it, the more it hurts, and the more it hurts the less we want to do it. We feel like it would be a lot less painful to just remain the way we are, but at the same time we don't like who we are.

Given that our beliefs are like a brick wall, the feelings we hold inside that support our beliefs are like the mortar that holds the bricks in place. By letting go of the feelings that support unwanted beliefs, there's nothing to hold them in place. Without the mortar, the bricks will eventually fall, leaving room for new beliefs to come forth.

To sum it up, affirmations are used correctly when the intention is to recondition the mind to be accepting—to create a more resourceful outlook. They are used incorrectly when the intention is to avoid or push away what are perceived as unpleasant feelings and emotional experiences.

A belief cannot be abandoned, changed or transformed until the supporting and underlying suppressed feelings have been cleared.

It is a well-known fact that our thoughts actually determine the direction we take in our lives, and for this reason most self-improvement programs focus on changing one's mind. However, it is not well-known that the feelings we hold from the past actually create the outcomes in our lives. As an example, if a person is hanging on to a feeling of anger or resentment from a breakup or hurt from a past relationship, until the feeling is released he or she will continue to attract similar circumstances supporting that feeling, thereby keeping it alive in the present.

Look at it this way. Feelings are an energy that we continually project upon the outside world. We will see and experience only what we are projecting. If we are hanging on to anger, we will continually be faced with situations that will provide us with the opportunity to let go and move past our anger. Until we deal with it and let it go, it will surface again and again. We project what we feel, and we attract what we project. The expectations of others, the standards they expect us to live up to, are really our own projections. We judge ourselves by our standards, project them out to other people and then believe they think those things about us. Let's say that you are depressed and you judge yourself for being depressed. You look at your friends and think they hate it when you are depressed; you think they are judging you, when in fact they may not have any reaction at all. They may not even notice. It is your own standards that aren't being met.

What if your friend does notice your depression and judges you for it? Well, that's their problem, not yours, just as it would be your problem if you hated their depression. Whoever sees the problem owns it. It's in *their* head!

Who we are, the relationships we experience with those in our lives, and the circumstances we are living are based solely upon our beliefs, and the feelings that we hang on to that keep the beliefs alive.

The secret to living a successful and happy life is to build up an emotional conviction from the heart of what we want, and then to let go of that which no longer supports that conviction. We will attract only what we project.

Everything in our lives comes to us, or is repelled from us, based upon the vibration of our own energy field. And that energy field is established by our beliefs and feelings, and the resulting convictions and behaviors they collectively produce. As an example, think of a time when you were around someone who was angry, anxious or desperate about a situation in his or her life. How did you feel when you were around them? Did it give you a comforting, resourceful feeling, or did it start to bring you down as well? How about being confronted by a pushy salesperson the last time you made a major purchase? Did it give you a feeling that you could trust that person or a feeling of distrust?

Once we fully understand this concept, we will see that nothing is truly out of place in our lives, and that everything is perfect based upon our level of consciousness. The world is simply a mirror of our convictions (beliefs and feelings) stamped out in material form.

Do you like what you see? Do you like the world you have created for yourself? We are our own architect and our own builder. We have built our world to the exact specifications of our own beliefs and feelings.

Even if we ran away from home, our current job or our circle of friends, even if we ran away from our present lifestyle with the thought of starting over in another state, in time we would create an almost exact duplication of our former world. We simply cannot run away from our world—because we cannot run away from our beliefs and feelings—but we can change them, therefore changing our world.

If we truly want to change our experience of life, we must first change the rules by which we've been living.

As an example, if someone gives us money to help us take care of a financial lack, if we don't change the rules that got us where we are, if we don't change how we feel about money, we'll soon be back in the same situation. The situation will simply return when enough tension builds up again as a result of our suppressed feelings and beliefs about money. In other words, if at the end of each month a person doesn't have the money to pay their mortgage payment, they could borrow the money to pay it. However, borrowing the money doesn't solve their real problem. They need to examine what they believe about money (or the lack of it) because that is what put them there in the first place.

Happiness Is Not Eluding You

In order for our world to improve, our underlying belief about how we perceive the world must change. In order to change a belief, the trapped feeling that keeps it alive must be released. A new awareness must then be developed from within as to what happiness really is. We must develop a new understanding about our own true nature. In order to do this, we must develop a new understanding, not of happiness, but rather of what causes unhappiness.

Happiness is not eluding us. It's our idea about happiness that eludes us. We should seek to give up incorrect ideas instead of giving up our happiness. Happiness can only exist when we begin to see that our unhappiness is not connected to an event itself, but rather to how we perceive the event. The simple key to happiness is to develop the ability to let go of the feelings we've trapped inside that are no longer supportive of how we would like our lives to be. We must not only let go of those feelings associated with old hurts, pains and mistakes, but those we encounter as part of our daily lives as well.

We all make unsuccessful attempts to let go by avoiding, expressing or ignoring our feelings, or we try to push ahead despite our feelings. It's an exhausting battle, one that can't be won by force. Using force will only end up causing us to suppress our feelings even deeper, allowing them to return again later.

Suppressing a feeling is like driving our car with one foot on the brake and the other on the gas. We feel stuck, caught in an endless cycle of frustration, going nowhere. To top it off, we live in a society that denies the whole problem. Denial, of course, is just another form of suppression. Denial won't make anything go away. Letting go is the key. Everyone has the inborn ability to let go of nonsupportive feelings and move on. It's simply a matter of choice. It's a choice to let go and grow, or to hang on and stay stuck where we are. Real and permanent growth occurs in our lives only when we release a nonsupportive feeling.

A woman called me recently who had just read my book *Rings of Truth*. She said that as a result of what she learned from it, she discovered some things she was hanging on to in the form of resentment toward her mother. She explained that the two of them hadn't spoken for almost twenty years. She said that after she let go of her resentment, she and her mother began communicating on a regular basis. She was amazed at how much growth had occurred for her simply by letting go. She was also surprised by how little effort it required on her part to let go and move past her issue.

Letting go requires no effort, only choice. The real effort comes from hanging on!

Many kinds of growth therapies are available, and some are very worthwhile. However, any therapy that leads us to believe that our life is awful or we are awful because of something we did, or something that someone else did to us, is at the very least incomplete. We've all had a lot done to us, and we've all done a lot to ourselves. None of that matters! It's all in the past. None of it is happening to us now. We are all perfect just the way we are. All we really need to do is to let go of the nonsupportive feelings trapped inside that cause us to believe that we are less than perfect.

The only thing for which we truly need to take responsibility is right here, right now. We need to take total responsibility for how we feel right now. What else is there except right now? We should blame no one for our circumstances or lack of happiness, and that includes ourselves. In order to experience true growth, we must take responsibility for experiencing life the way it is now, this very moment, not how it used to be or how we want it to be. Nothing else exists except this moment. This moment is where happiness exists. There is nothing we can have any effect on except this very moment.

Self-Observation Is Seeing Truth

I'm always reminded of two statements from the Bible. One is, "And one day time will be no more." This simply means, "Some day we will live in the present." The other is, "Many are called, but few are chosen," which means, "Few listen."

Self-observation is the real key to listening and seeing truth. Letting go is the key to living in the present. Letting go of what makes us unhappy is the key to happiness. What else could do more? We can't chase away the past, and we can't grab hold of the future. Letting go and living in the moment is the only way to find happiness. If there is another way, I'd sure like to know about it.

So what do we let go of? We let go of all the emotional distress that drags us through all our unpleasant experiences. Letting go allows us to set our mental clock back to zero, where we can live our lives without looking through the filters of yesterday's mistakes or tomorrow's worries.

Maybe you don't believe that letting go will really work for you. Belief plays no part in letting go. You don't have to believe it works in order for it to work. Getting you to believe me doesn't concern me at all. I do know one thing, though: it won't do you any harm to practice letting go. Who knows, it just might work! If you give it a test for the next thirty days and it doesn't work for you, what have you lost? Nothing. It doesn't even require any additional time on your part to try it. If it doesn't work, you'll still be right where you are right now.

The important point is, if you don't give it a try, then you'll never know if it would have worked.

We can all spend years in counseling, therapy, attending seminars, going to spiritual retreats or looking for some guru to enlighten us, but until we make a conscious choice to do it differently, we'll just keep right on going around in our circles looking for a way out.

Everyone has blocks, destructive habit patterns, stresses and addictions that keep them in pain. Even physical symptoms can be linked to emotional distresses, both directly and indirectly. Emotional distress is a warning signal, an alarm clock telling us it's time to wake up, to let go. The main purpose for letting go is to help us activate growth and to experience more self-love and happiness. Whatever it is that we think we need in order to be happy is nothing less than emotional self-healing.

Five critical elements come to mind as necessary for self-healing and growth.

1. Concern: Concern means caring enough about yourself to be interested in taking the time to explore with

an open mind what might be done to facilitate emotional self-healing and growth in a whole new way.

2. Willingness: For self-healing, you must have the willingness to be self-observant, to put into practice the principles outlined in this book and to give them a try before making any judgments as to whether they will work for you.

3. Patience: Patience is required for the necessary clearing and rebalancing of your system. We have been emotionally abusing ourselves for a long time through hanging on to and suppressing our feelings. We shouldn't expect overnight results, even though we may see some right away.

4. Nurturing: Nurturing is the first step toward loving yourself. It will activate your heart and let you feel your true, loving self once again. When you open your heart, the real you will step forward and take center stage.

5. Courage: Courage is required to face and own your circumstances instead of blaming external conditions. With courage you'll begin to feel your warrior spirit emerge as you face and let go of your fears. Without courage, fear will take over and run your life. Once you've let go of your fears, you'll find that you no longer need courage. Courage is only needed when fear is present. Without fear, courage simply becomes a natural act.

Everyday application is the key. The principles and insights ahead of you, when practiced daily, will truly let you live within your authentic power. Resistance-free living can open the door to the new life you've always dreamed of. You'll begin to discover your forgotten ability to "let go" and live in that place of happiness, despite your circumstances.

There is no better time than now to be happy. If not now, when? Your life will always be filled with challenges. All you have to do is to decide to unlearn your old ways. You may feel that your life is just about to get better as soon as a certain thing happens, but there will always be obstacles in the way, something you have to get through first before you can be happy.

To have happiness, you must be willing to open yourself up to pain. When you open to pain, you also open to joy. When you take off those rose-colored glasses, the first person you see will be someone you love . . . yourself!

Obstacles are a part of life. Getting rid of obstacles is not the way to find happiness. Happiness is the way. Treasure every moment. Time waits for no one. Don't wait for happiness until you get the right job, find the right mate, lose ten pounds, until the kids are grown, until the kids leave home, until you get divorced, until you retire, until summer, until you have a drink, until you have enough money, until you die, or until you are born again and discover that there's no better time than right now to be happy. Happiness is a journey, not a destination.

2

Letting Go

*Letting go
of whatever
is wrong
in your life
must
always precede
attracting
what is right*

What if you owned a factory? Let's say that you manufactured beautiful dining-room furniture. What would you need to do? You would probably need a clear vision of the product you wanted to produce. You would have a set of plans showing how to build the furniture. You would probably have a goal as to how many pieces you were going to build in a given period of time. So, you would have a vision, a plan, and a goal, and of course you'd have the finished product. You would also need a warehouse full of raw materials and a manufacturing facility. Your warehouse would be full of wood, paint, sandpaper, pegs, brackets, casters, shipping crates and all the other materials needed to build your furniture. You would also need a workplace where you assembled the furniture and a place where you discarded all the waste materials—all the paint cans, wood shavings, pieces of wood, worn-out sandpaper, etc.

What would happen if you didn't toss out the waste for a day? You might still be able to function. What about waiting for two days? How about three, a week or a month? Eventually it would be very difficult to get around and work efficiently, wouldn't it? Eventually, if you didn't clean the waste out of your workplace, you'd be out of business, wouldn't you?

Now let's look at the human body. Our bodies are like a factory. In our factory, we all have a vision of how we would like to look and feel. Our vision would probably be one of health, peace of mind and vitality.

We attempt to take care of ourselves as best we can. We stock our kitchen with the best raw materials—food, drink, vitamins, etc. We consume all the raw materials we need in hopes of achieving our vision of health and vitality. Our bodies then digest and assimilate the food, water and other nutrients from our chosen sources, in order to keep our vital organs healthy and vibrant. And of course, just like the furniture factory, our bodies give off waste.

What do you think would happen to your body, your personal factory, if you didn't get rid of the waste? At first you'd probably get a little uncomfortable, unable to perform at your optimal level, similar to working in the factory with waste piled high. Next, you might start feeling a little tired, because your body is working harder than it should. Next, sickness would set in. Eventually, if you never eliminated the waste, you'd be out of business. In other words, your body would die.

What about your mental factory? Your emotional factory? Do you think we have waste we need to get rid of? We sure do, and lots of it!

We all have a vision of how we would like our lives to be. We all basically want some of the same things. We want to be happy, to be well-balanced and to have peace of mind.

Our mental factory also utilizes raw materials. However, the whole world becomes our warehouse of raw materials, as well as our workshop. We get our raw materials from many sources—our work environment, family, the books we read, the people with whom we associate, newspapers, television, mail, personal experiences, relaxation, noise, fun time, nature, etc.

Within the time span of a few minutes, we can hear about the latest weight-loss craze. Lose twenty-nine pounds in thirty days! Someone famous commits suicide! Aliens spotted over New Jersey! The top ten investments to attain financial freedom. We have a hundred decisions to make in our business. We have to decide what the best use of our money might be. We have to think about the family, our relationships and our health. We hear about wars, riots, murders, etc., all of which are attempting to create an emotional response within us to get us to pay attention. We also have a lot of good material from which to make our choices. Yet, much of the input we receive every day, or 'raw material,' is designed to create a negative emotional response. When was the last time you saw good news on the television or in the newspaper? It's rarely seen because good news doesn't sell.

So, here we are with all this raw material to choose from to produce a happy, joyful life. We gather the raw material, process it, decide what we want to utilize and eliminate the rest. Right? Wrong! We leave a lot more lying around than we need, just in case we need it for later.

What about all those past mistakes, pains, hurts and failures? Well, we never know when we might need one of them to protect us from that ever happening again. What about that time when you got fired from your job? You don't want to let that anger toward your former boss go, do you? What about that failed marriage? Don't want to repeat that one again, do you? Better hang on to that one for sure! We want to remember all the sad details, so we won't find ourselves in another situation like that.

What about that time you had to file bankruptcy, or when you saw your parents fighting when you were a child? Don't want to let that go, do you? To top it off, you have in a day's time more information that needs processing coming through your mental factory than you could effectively handle in a week.

Eliminating Emotional Waste

What happens over time if we don't eliminate the waste from our mental and emotional factories?

Here's what happens: stress, loneliness, anxiety, worry, depression, fear, exhaustion, time pressure, doubt, feelings of being victimized or out of control. Could the excess emotional waste that we don't let go of cause these kinds of responses? Could it take its toll on our happiness and peace of mind? Could it affect us physically, causing responses such as high blood pressure, heart attacks and the like? You bet it can, and it does!

Here's the problem we all face. Our lives have become much too complicated compared to a couple of thousand years ago or even fifty to seventy-five years ago, when we received an hour of input, and we had a week to process it. Today, it's a little more intense. We receive a week's worth of input in a single day, and we have only an hour to process it. The solution is to learn to quickly recognize and to let go of those thoughts, feelings, emotions and behaviors that no longer support your vision of how you want your life to be. If reading the newspaper in the morning supports you, then you should read it. If it does not, then you should let it go. If the upset you had at the office this morning, yesterday or last week supports your life and makes it better, hang on to it. If not, why not let it go?

We want to have our lives work better, yet we continue to hang on to those things that keep us in a nonresourceful, unhappy state. Which is more productive, the action we take from a position of upset and nonresourcefulness, or the action we take from being resourceful? In other words, is it more productive to take action from a clear mind and an open heart, or through the filters of yesterday's upset?

We will discuss later what it means to stand back and observe our behaviors and circumstances. Here's an example: If we were creating an arrangement of roses, at some point we'd step back and observe, maybe move a flower or two, until we got it just the way we wanted it.

We observe ourselves while combing our hair, getting dressed, etc., but do we truly look at ourselves? Begin to look at yourself as you hang on to your own drama. Watch yourself as you hang on to feeling sorry for yourself, as you cling to all those personal problems, as you feel stressed as a result of your need to be right, or to control how someone else is acting. Watch yourself as you feel you have to be in control. Observe yourself as you hang on to that state of anger as a form of protection in order to avoid some pain. That's what I mean by hanging on to your drama.

We say we want to be free of our problems, but the real truth is we don't! In fact, we love our problems, and we love our drama. We want to complain about how awful things are, what other people did to us, how broke we are and how life is not fair. We unconsciously want to feel the way we do in order to justify not taking responsibility for where we are in life.

A Question of Honor

The real question we should ask ourselves is this: "Which do I honor more, the life I really want to live, or my circumstances, my drama?" We always, and with mathematical accuracy, attract what we most honor.

I recently had a call from an acquaintance telling me that he was thinking of getting involved in a new home-based business. He knew that I taught a course for entrepreneurs, and he wanted to know if I thought it would be a viable business. I told him that I believed it would, and that I thought he would be very good at it. I asked him when he planned to get started. He said that he was going to get started in his new business just as soon as he tied up some loose ends. He shared with me how excited he was about all that he planned to accomplish once he got involved. I asked him what he had to do before he could begin. He said that he had all these problems he had to take care of first. He explained that the IRS was after him for back taxes. He was going through a divorce, and there was a possibility that his job would not last much longer, among several other things. It was a depressing list of reasons, or rather, excuses. He said that just as soon as he took care of all those things, he was then going to get started in his new business and create the new life he wanted.

I asked if he would mind if I asked him a question, to which he answered, "No." So I asked him, "Which do you honor the most, your vision of how you would like your life to be, or your circumstances?" His answer was, "I honor my vision the most, of course." So, I said, "Then why are you going to wait to get started with your new business until all your problems are resolved?" He then said, "I just told you why I can't." Then he proceeded to go back through his list of reasons why he had to wait. I said, "So, what you're telling me is that you honor your 'stuff' more than your new life plan. What you are telling me is that you honor the IRS, the divorce you are going through and the possibility of losing your job more than your vision."

Again, we always act upon and attract into our lives what we honor the most. What we will have in our future will always be based upon what we honor the most in the present. And what we have in the present is totally based upon what we have honored in our past, nothing more, nothing less. The more we let go of and cease to honor our distresses, the less we need to complain about how things are, and the more productive we become. Besides, when we finally get through with our problems, there will be a whole new set of problems to appear in their place. There will always be things that we're dealing with that we can use as an excuse for not doing well, not following our dreams, not getting started today or not being happy. If we wait until all our problems are resolved before we take action, we will always be waiting, because all of our problems will never be resolved.

Letting go of the feelings and emotions that keep us stuck is the answer. If we find ourselves needing acceptance from others, we haven't let go. We are honoring our need for acceptance more than our peace of mind. If we discover we have a need to control others, we haven't let go. If we observe ourselves wanting others to see us in a certain way, we haven't let go. The more we make a conscious effort to let go, the more we'll begin to discover who we really are and what we really want in our lives. Letting go of what's wrong in our lives must always be ahead of attracting what's right. Letting go is always a choice. We justify hanging on in order to keep pretending that we are not responsible for how we feel, or that our feelings are all caused by some outside circumstance.

Our lives are not about the lessons we think we are here to learn, as most people believe. Our lives are about discovering who we really are. It's about uncovering our true nature. Waking up to who we are requires letting go of that which we imagine ourselves to be. When we begin to let go of what is false, we automatically exist in what is true. Our true nature doesn't have to hang on to anything, or learn anything, because it already *is* everything.

There will always be incompetent and irresponsible people. There may always be a lack of money, good jobs, vacations and opportunities. There will always be all sorts of unexpected circumstances. The traffic will always be too heavy. There will always be rainy days and Mondays. We may not have a choice about what sometimes gets handed to us in life, but here's what we do have a choice about. We have a choice about how we handle what is handed to us, what we do about our circumstance.

Resolving Unresolved Experiences

Most of us keep our minds in a state of immobility. Our minds are on hold, like a telephone with ten lines, all blinking at once, all waiting for us to answer! There's so much going on that we don't know what to do or which line to answer.

We don't know who to talk to first. So what do we do? We avoid the ones we don't want to handle right now and put them on hold until later. Just like a multiple-line telephone system, our brain is holding all the unresolved experiences— all taking up space, all creating certain kinds of feelings and giving us the same messages over and over, influencing our every behavior.

We put off or repress the messages we don't want to deal with, dodging the ones that might cause us pain or discomfort. There's a line holding for every person we haven't forgiven. There's one holding for every emotional hurt that we've encountered and haven't resolved. There's a line holding for literally every unresolved experience we've had in our lives. Because of all the pressure created by all the lines we have on hold and haven't resolved, we take an automatic position based upon past programming on most of the current issues in our lives.

Let's say you're in sales. You're making a sales call, but you're still hanging on to the "no" that you received from your past four calls. Here you are making your new sales call while looking through the filters of the past. The real question is this: Does hanging on support your vision of making an effective sales call and a new sale? No, of course not! Why? It's because you are taking action from a place of fear or nonresourcefulness, and that is what you'll attract more of in return.

Perhaps you are entering into a new relationship, hoping

it will be better than the last one. At the same time, you are holding on to the hurt from the last relationship. You're hanging on to and remembering past experience so that you won't make the same mistake again. But really you're going into the new relationship looking through self-created filters from the last experience, the past programming of failure or hurt. The chance of making the next relationship better with this approach is roughly zero percent. Why? Because we always get that which we honor the most. We attract what we are projecting out to the world. And what we are projecting in this case is fear!

So, the questions are, *How do we resolve the issue? How do we reduce the number of lines on hold? How do we let go? How do we stop the pain? How do we experience more love in our lives? How do we accept others? How do we let go of the past without losing control of our lives in the present?*

How did you learn to walk, ride a bicycle, swim or drive a car? For that matter, how did you learn to read the words you are reading right now? Did someone tell you what takes place in your brain in order to learn to read? Did someone tell you what takes place in your body in order to take a single step? Did someone explain to you how each muscle and tendon must work in concert, and how messages must come from your brain in order to start the process? Or one day perhaps you just up and said, "I've had it with all this crawling around—I'm going to learn to walk!" One day you just decided that you were going to ride a bicycle, read a book or drive a car. You instinctively knew that the only way you were going to do these things was to simply do them.

Letting go is just like learning to do any of these things. Four things are required to let go: self-observation, intention, willingness and commitment. If we choose to hang on to our old ways, it requires the lack of self-observation, intention, willingness and commitment.

We let go of things every day. All we really need to do is to become more conscious of the process and not to complicate it. Being more conscious means becoming more self-observant.

I suppose you could live with nonresourceful emotions for a while longer, but I don't think you'll really want to hang on to them for the rest of your life, will you? The fact that you are reading this book tells me you are tired of how you are feeling and the results you are producing. Is that not true?

We must be willing to tune in, observe our feelings and determine which feel painful and which feel pleasant. Then we must consciously choose to let go of the nonsupportive ones through intention, willingness and commitment. We have to intend to let the feeling go; we have to be willing to let it go; and we must commit to letting it go. Most important of all is to become more self-observant of how we feel, and to ask ourselves, "Is this feeling supportive or nonsupportive?"

Let's say, for example, that you find yourself in an abusive or unfulfilling relationship. Ask yourself, "Do I like feeling this way? Do I want to let it go? Am I willing to let it go?"

And the most important question of all is, "When?" As soon as you make a conscious choice to let go of your need for acceptance, the relationship will begin to heal, one way or the other. And however it turns out, the most important thing is that you have healed.

Feelings Are Trapped Energy Patterns

There's nothing mysterious about feelings and emotions, or about letting them go, once we truly understand what they are in the first place. This fear, anger, sadness, doubt, etc., is nothing more than trapped energy patterns that have developed through our past experiences. Think about it. If we didn't have a past, would we have doubts, fears and anger? No, of course we wouldn't. If we had no past, we would have no emotions, because emotions are created from feelings trapped in place as a result of our past experiences.

Most of the time we think of events as having a starting point and an ending. But do they really? What about the words you are reading right now? Stop reading for a minute. Where are the words you just read? They really don't exist anymore, do they? When you've finished the whole book, where is it? Where are the words? There are no words anymore. All that's left are the memory patterns that were put there by the spell that was cast by the sound of the words as you repeated them in your mind. All that is left are the memory patterns and the feelings created by the impact of the words you've just read. The memory patterns are at best incomplete. We remember only the words and concepts that impact us in some way, thus creating a feeling.

When we organize a group of letters in a certain sequence, it creates a word. We call that "spelling." Think about the word *spelling*. What do you think it means? Spelling is the organization and structuring of letters into a word. Another definition is "to cast a spell." When we organize a group of letters into a certain sequence, and speak the word to someone else, we actually cast a spell on its receiver. It also casts a spell on the one transmitting it. Even when we think a thought about someone else, that word in our thought casts a spell on the sender as well as the receiver. That's right, even a thought you think toward another has its effect. The thought casts its spell.

Now, what about the word *sentence*? A sentence is the organization of a series of spelled words. So the power of a sentence is much stronger than a single word by itself. It doesn't just cast a spell; it pronounces a sentence. As an example, when in a state of emotional rage you yell at a child, you may sentence that child to a life of emotional scars that may never heal. At the same time, the yelling further suppresses the anger of the sender. How do you think we got our programs, all the dramas that we're dealing with today? We remain prisoners of our own programming. "Our sentence" will require us to be locked up in our own jail until we make a conscious choice to take a different approach. The questions should always be: Is the language I'm using—the spell I'm casting—empowering or disempowering? Is the feeling I'm hanging on to, or the emotion I'm experiencing, moving me closer to or further away from what I would love to have in my life?

Everything Has a Beginning, a Middle and an Ending

Try this exercise: recall a past upset. Maybe a conflict or an argument you had with someone. Next, think about when it began. Remember when the tension or upset first began. Now, recall when you felt the most intense about the issue. Let's call that the middle. And last, recall when it was over and you were relaxed once again (if it is actually over).

Now, ask yourself how long it took from the first upset to the ending, or until now if it's not yet over. We may have experienced an upset this morning at the office, and by now it is gone. We've let it go. On the other hand, I've had people in my workshops who have been hanging on to an upset for thirty to forty years and more! They refuse to let it go. They either have intention, willingness, and commitment to let it go, or they have intention, willingness, and commitment to hang on. And in some cases they may want to let it go, but they don't know that they can or how simple it is to do so. In some cases they want to let it go, but they aren't willing to do so.

Many people are actually afraid to let go. They believe that letting go is being passive, and that they'll get walked on. Letting go is not being passive at all. Letting go is about taking action. It's about taking action from a state of resourcefulness rather than nonresourcefulness, from a place of love versus fear. It's impossible to take resourceful action if we're stuck by hanging on to a nonresourceful feeling or belief system about something or someone. It's impossible to experience self-love when we're hanging on to self-hate. It always comes down to the question of honor. We often find it difficult to let go, because every time the feeling comes up, and we think about it or speak it, we are casting a new spell and renewing the sentence that we've placed upon ourselves in the first place, by hanging on.

Which is more productive? Is it better to take action from upset, or action from resourcefulness? By letting go of the upset, we can then see more clearly the real situation and what needs to be done to resolve it—not what would make us feel good, or keep us from some temporary pain, but what the right solution is for all involved. In other words, without first letting go of the old, we can't see reality; we aren't open for the right solution.

Breaking the Chain of Pain

Hanging on to an upset creates a connection between you and that event or person. It creates a chain of pain. When we hang on to an old upset we've had with another, we create a nonresourceful feeling inside us; we are "out of source." At the same time, we cause the same energy to flow toward the person with whom we're upset, thus creating a chain of pain.

What's really happening when we hang on is that we create a vibrational harmony with that condition, which in turn creates more of the same. Until the chain is broken, we will continue to respond again and again in the same way. This will continue until we take responsibility and break the chain. Letting go breaks the chain of pain.

Anything we cling to will eventually cause us pain. Let's say you are in the habit of having a cup of coffee every morning when you first get up. What if one morning you didn't have your cup of coffee? What happens around 10:00 A.M.? Right, a headache, a withdrawal symptom. Anything we cling to will eventually cause us pain.

A few years ago a woman in my workshop shared with the group that twenty years prior she had had a bitter argument with her mother, which had resulted in her mother not speaking to her for the past twenty years. She had tried numerous times to make amends, but her mother wouldn't respond. She would call and leave messages and write letters, but her mother wouldn't answer the messages or the letters. The daughter shared how upset she was with her mother, how much she loved her, and at the same time, how angry she was toward her. She was deeply hurt that her mother would no longer have anything to do with her.

I worked with the woman for about fifteen minutes,

helping her let go of the feelings and emotions she had toward her mother. This was on Saturday, the first day of the seminar, around three o'clock in the afternoon. The next day when she arrived at class, she was overwhelmed with joy! She shared with the group that upon arriving at home around six o'clock she checked her messages, and to her surprise, she had one from her mother after twenty years of no contact. Her mother said, "I was just thinking that this anger has gone on between us long enough. Could we get together and resolve the issue?" And guess what time the message came in from her mother? It was shortly after 3:00 P.M. Within minutes after she had let go of her resentment toward her mother in the class, her mother felt the break in the chain of pain. What happened was that the woman in the seminar finally took responsibility for her own feelings toward her mother, and when she did, the chain of pain between her and her mother was broken.

All she really needed to do was take responsibility for how she felt, not how her mother felt, and to let go of her own resentment and anger toward her mother.

To let go simply means to be open to other possibilities, to let alone, to loose one's hold of, to behave in an unrestrained way. Letting go sets our emotional (e-motion = "energy in motion") counter back to zero. You are taking the nonresourceful energy out of motion. Why would we want to get back to zero? At zero point, we can just be. We can connect with people without the filters of past experiences or the fears of the future that keep popping up in our minds. We get hurt by others not because of what they say or do, but because we demand that they do as we expect. When we let go of our demands, people can then act as they wish, and at the same time, we can remain at peace.

Those old pop-ups or inner dialogs prevent us from truly being in the present and really connecting with the other person. In most of our relationships we connect with others through our roles, our filters within our own dramas; in other words, who we want others to think we are versus who we really are. The main reason we sometimes feel disconnected from others is because all our "stuff" gets in the way of being who we really are. Letting go and getting to point zero allows us to truly connect with another, true nature to true nature, heart to heart. True love, true intimacy only operates in the present. Letting go of the past and the future leaves only now. Love only operates in the moment.

Letting Go of Control to Gain Control

Instead of just living our life as it is, we spend most of our time and energy keeping our stuff alive by trying to control everything. That's probably why we're so tired all the time. When we feel a need to control a situation, we remain out of control. However, when we let go of our need to be in control, we are now in complete control. When we detach ourselves from a nonresourceful feeling, we also detach ourselves from the stress it causes in our lives. One moment of letting go is worth more to our growth than a thousand hours of intellectual information and stimulation.

Many believe that letting go is an anxious pursuit to find new solutions to problems. On the contrary, letting go is not a pursuit at all. Letting go creates space for new solutions to come to us. When we're in hot pursuit to find answers, we are in a nonresourceful state, a state of chasing solutions or pushing solutions away, stifling our imagination and creativity. Letting go lets you live in the moment, where the action is and where the solutions are.

Letting go is resourcefulness.
Letting go is living in a state of love.
Letting go lets you do what you do with love.
Letting go is raising more empowered children.
Letting go lets you enjoy a more fulfilling relationship.
Letting go lets you be more productive at the office.
Letting go lets you live a healthier life.
Letting go lets you live free of stress.
Letting go lets you be the true person that you are.

Our inner emotional world is really no different from our outer physical world. As an example, if we severely cut our hand, we wouldn't just sit around trying to figure out why we caused this to happen, what our lesson was in all this, or what the real meaning was behind it. We wouldn't just let it bleed and do nothing about it so that we would clearly remember our lesson. No! We would go to the doctor, get some stitches and stop the bleeding, and we'd probably go as fast as we could.

The first message is very clear: "My hand is severely cut." And the second message is, "Take action right now to stop the bleeding!" The very same thing should apply to an inner hurt. Heal the pain first by letting go, *then* if we want to analyze it, go ahead. Of course once we let go we'll have no reason to analyze it. Why? Because the problem will probably be gone, and if it's not we can now take resourceful action to solve it. The only reason we feel compelled to analyze it is because it hurts. And it hurts only because we're hanging on and analyzing it! Letting go is a choice. Of course *not* letting go is also a choice. *I can't,* or *I don't have time to let go* is how we justify or pretend that we're not responsible for how we feel or the choices we make.

It takes no effort at all to let go. It's simple and natural. It's like a tree shedding its leaves in the fall; they drop what they no longer need in order to make room for the new in the spring.

Right now, think of something that you're hanging on to: an old hurt, resentment, anger because of an argument, fear or worry. Get in touch with how that makes you feel. Notice where you feel the feeling in your body. Let it grow in strength. Let the e-motion come forth. Now consider the following questions:

1. *Do I like feeling this way?* That's self-observation.

2. *Do I want to let it go?* That's intention.
3. *Am I willing to let it go?* That's willingness.
4. *When am I willing to let it go?* That's commitment.

If you hesitated on any of these questions, you need to go back, observe the feeling once again and reconsider until you are sure that you don't like feeling that way. Some do. They feel it provides them with some sort of protection that will keep the event from happening again or keep them in control. You have to be sure also that you want to let it go. I've talked with people who absolutely refuse to want to let it go. You have to want to. Otherwise, there is no way to let go. Are you willing to let it go? This becomes a little tougher. Being willing says you are willing to take responsibility for what's happening in your life. And the final question is, when? That's the really hard one. When are you willing to let it go? That's making a commitment to do it now, and never again blame an outside circumstance for how you are feeling. First comes observation, then the key words are *want to, willing to* and *when*! Self-observation, intention, willingness and commitment.

If your answer is yes, you want to let it go; and yes, you are willing to let it go; and yes, you are willing to do it now, you have just let go of all or at least part of the feeling.

Again, letting go requires intention, willingness and commitment. In fact, doing anything requires intention, willingness and commitment. Letting go or hanging on to a nonresourceful feeling always requires those same three ingredients. We must have the intention to hang on or to let go, the willingness to hang on or to let go, and the commitment to hang on or to let go. There's only one major difference in hanging on or letting go. Letting go requires no energy at all, whereas hanging on requires a lot!

Imagine for a moment how much time is required to travel 250,000 light years—that's traveling at the speed of light, 186,000 miles per second, for 250,000 years. That's hard to imagine, isn't it? A single galaxy is estimated to be that far across. Now imagine a galaxy that is four galaxies away from Earth. That's 1,000,000 light years away. Imagine that there are billions of galaxies within the universe. It's hard to imagine, isn't it?

Now imagine in the center of our galaxy is planet Earth. Compared to the whole, Earth is pretty small stuff, right? Now imagine yourself on Earth. Even smaller stuff, aren't you? Now imagine the problems that you try so hard to control. Pretty small stuff.

I have a theory. When we arrive here on Earth, we are given an allotment of "cosmic energy" to burn up, and when it's gone, our trip gets canceled. We choose how we burn up our energy.

Let's say you are traveling down the freeway at sixty miles per hour. You're going to an appointment five miles away, and if you continue at the same speed, you'll arrive on time. All of a sudden you get cut off by someone who decides to travel at only fifty-five miles per hour. You begin to get uptight. *How*

could this idiot be in front of me? Doesn't he have a brain or what?
If you continue at the same speed for the remainder of your
five miles, that "idiot" will have cost you about thirty seconds.

The thirty seconds is not the issue. The real issue is how
much of your cosmic energy allotment you have used. To
what degree did your need to control something that is not
within your control shorten your time on Earth?

Imagine this: you go into the bathroom and at the critical
moment realize there's no toilet tissue. You have a choice to
make. Do you want to burn up some of your cosmic energy
allotment for this? It's alright if you do, but it's really good to
know who's making the decisions.

You are having an argument with your spouse and you're
getting pretty angry. You might want to consider two things.
First, you might want to ask yourself, *Who really wins in an
argument?* The second thing is, *Do I want to burn a portion of my
energy allotment for this, or is there a more sane, stress-free solution?*

We suffer physically when something is not working properly in our bodies. We suffer emotionally when something is
not working in concert with our beliefs. We suffer mentally
when we don't get what we want, or when we feel forced to
live with something we don't want. Any type of suffering
shortens our time here on Earth by burning up our allotment
of cosmic energy. That's my theory.

If we didn't hang on and experience something as nonresourceful, would it be? Think about it. Anything that we
become attached to—a belief, a nonresourceful feeling,

anything we are determined to be right about—will be an area in which our inner peace is affected. I remember years ago being hooked on that morning cup of coffee. If I didn't have it by around ten in the morning, I would have a withdrawal headache by eleven. I must have quit drinking coffee a hundred times. I had the intention and willingness, but I never truly quit until the day I made the commitment. Anything we become attached to will eventually cause us pain. We can become attached to feeling a certain way. We could become attached to anger for example, and feel that if we let it go, a part of us would die as well. Some attachments cause more pain than others. The attachment we have toward those we love is a lifelong attachment and as a result is much harder to let go. When a loved one dies, we feel as if a part of us dies as well. We feel pain, heartache and sadness, but eventually we deal with the loss and move forward with our lives, savoring the memories of the past.

I remember a woman in one of my workshops who had lost her son about fifteen years before. She refused to let it go. She wanted to hang on to the sadness she felt, hoping in some way it might bring him back. I worked with her on letting go of her attachment, assuring her that her special memories wouldn't be lost as well. After some time she finally let it go. When she did, she stood up crying tears of joy, repeating over and over, "I finally let him go! I finally let him go!"

For more than fifteen years she had been unwilling to face

the truth that her son was dead and there was nothing she could do about it. As a result, she spent over fifteen years not living her own life fully. Anything we become attached to will eventually cause us pain, whether it's an emotion, feeling, physical addiction, money or other material things, a person, a job, etc.

Our prison lies within us. It's in our hearts and minds. We lock ourselves in self-made chains of pain. Pain and suffering are based on ignorance. We don't see our situation for what it is, and by not doing so, we can't see how to deal with it. We are blinded to solutions. We pass by the joys and happiness in life, not realizing we've missed a thing.

We are like a fish that is swimming toward a net knowing it will be trapped. But because of our unwillingness to see the truth, we continue heading in the same direction, hoping something will change before we are trapped in the net.

When we see the truth by observing that the net is there, we can simply lower the net and move forward with ease. The real problem is that we disregard what we see as being truth. We want our situation to be something other than what it is. We want to control something that is not within our control.

Finding Inner Peace

Inner peace, happiness, love and joy are connections to our own resourceful nature. In order to achieve inner peace we must have nothing to defend, nothing that we are attached to and no need to be right. A crisis only becomes a breaking point when we fail to use it as a turning point.

Letting go doesn't mean giving up control of our lives. Letting go simply means coming from a peaceful place inside.

Think of something in your life that you would like to feel peaceful about—something you've been hanging on to, something that you are attached to or something that causes you pain. Now, take a moment to get in touch with how it makes you feel. Observe yourself feeling the way you do. Now, say to yourself: "The only reason that I can't be at peace with this is . . ." and fill in the blank. What keeps you from being at peace with this issue? When you find out what keeps you from being at peace with this issue, you will have discovered what it is that you need to let go of.

Letting go puts your mind in a state of receptivity and at the same time provides you with an opportunity to see other issues that may need attention, relationships that need healing, past mistakes that need to be forgotten or resolved, and emotional wounds that need healing. New opportunities to resolve issues in our lives cannot come forth if the old is taking up all the space. It's necessary to let go of old beliefs, habits, opinions and even some friends in order to allow in the new.

Letting go doesn't require a lot of time, if any, whereas hanging on does. It consumes at least 90 percent of most people's time. If we don't handle nonresourceful feelings quickly, on the spot when they arise, we will always suppress or repress them, which in turn creates a pattern of behavior that will attract certain painful conditions once again.

When a feeling is released, four things are achieved. First, the suppressed feeling itself is weakened, or completely resolved. Second, the belief that supports the action pattern is eventually released. Third, the action pattern is weakened with every release of a feeling. And fourth, our happiness is increased. You can make yourself unhappy, but you can't make yourself happy. Why? Because, when it comes to being happy, any effort will be in vain. Why? Because we can't pursue happiness, it can't be possessed. Happiness is the natural by-product of letting go of those things that make us unhappy.

The most important thing to remember is to always deal first with the problems at hand. If a nonresourceful feeling is present, this represents an immediate problem that needs attention. By letting go and living in the present moment, we can simply observe our problems with silent strength, instead of being swept away by them.

When we make a choice not to let go, we are making a decision to chase the solutions, or rather, I should say, chase the problems. On the other hand, when we let go, we are detaching from the problem so that we can give birth to new solutions.

Learning to let go and simply have the courage to just leave it at that will leave us open to receive the solutions to our problems. Our biggest obstacle in life seems to be trying to figure out how to handle our problems rather than getting rid of them once and for all! Pushing forward, trying to forget our problems, is not only hanging on, but it's suppressing the issue, allowing it to return later even stronger. When we let go, everything seems different, even though nothing outside us has changed at all. The change actually took place inside, and all we did was stop resisting. When we stop resisting, we'll also find others around us not being resistant as well.

Another caution is not to attempt to analyze the feeling. Analyzing a feeling only strengthens it. The key is to simply observe the feeling, and let it go. Although many believe that expressing a feeling is required in order to let it go, that's not the case. Whenever we allow a feeling to become conscious without resistance, it begins to clear. Expression of a feeling such as anger only creates more resistance and actually enhances the feeling rather than resolving it.

It truly doesn't make any difference who is at fault in a given situation. The real point should be to solve the problem at hand, not to find fault. In most disagreements both parties are so busy blaming the other person and defending their own positions that they forget to solve the problem. Think about it. If an emotion such as anger didn't have any energy in it, would it be a problem? Of course not. If there were no energy in it, there would be no emotion at all. The trapped energy is the problem. If people would simply understand this fact, there would be no reason to fight because there would be nothing to win! There is nothing to become attached to except the emotion, derived from past experiences. A past experience has nothing to do with right here, right now. So why not just relax and let go? It certainly won't make matters any worse, and it just might make them better.

Begin to simply sit back and observe your own actions. Begin to experience emotions such as fear or anger as just energy that comes and goes. Just be observant without attempting to express or suppress the feeling. Simply observe it and let it be. Just observe it without letting it consume you, without identifying with it. Just observe it as "a" feeling rather than "your" feeling. In other words, *I am feeling anxious* rather than *I am anxious.* Just be with your feeling and allow your exploration of the feeling to go deeper. If there is a fear of letting go, then let go of the fears that keep you from letting go. Looking closer at any painful feeling or situation is the first step to letting go.

See your feeling like an onion, and know that each time you observe it, you are peeling off layers, one by one. When the layers are all peeled away, what do you think will be left? The real you, that's what! Experiencing more love in your life is an unlearning process, not a learning process.

When we allow ourselves to become motivated by a non-resourceful feeling by hanging on to it, what we are doing is actually reinforcing its power over us. When we do this we are also reinforcing the nonresourceful habit pattern, which allows it to return again at a later time with reinforcements! Perhaps if we would stop abusing ourselves by hanging on, there would be no reason to continue the type of behavior that leads to the self-abuse. We do not pay a large price for our development, but rather for clinging to our old ways.

I know this approach goes against our conditioning. Not reacting to a situation is difficult when we feel threatened and we want to defend ourselves. But what we'll find by letting go, by not reacting to a situation, is that our lives become much more effective in every way. The reason we become more effective by letting go is that our emotions are not in the way. In other words we can now take action from a place of clarity and resourcefulness.

Not reacting does not mean that we become passive to anyone's aggressions. We simply realize that if someone is upset with us, that his or her upset is not about us. Their upset is just the drama they are acting out, and we happened to be there at the time. We can choose to play a part in their drama . . . or not. Besides, if we want peace of mind, we will always be attracting those who upset us. Peace of mind won't arrive in a limousine as we might hope. Instead, we'll run into situation after situation that lets us practice not becoming involved and maintaining peace of mind. If we continue to hang on to all the nonpeaceful feelings and emotions, there will be no room for any sort of peace of mind in our lives.

If we want to have more money in our lives, and at the same time we are in a frantic pursuit for money, trying to do ten things at a time is not the answer. With that kind of anxiety toward money, there will be no capacity in our lives to attract it. In order to attract money, first and foremost, we have to let go of our anxiety toward money. Otherwise, all we attract is the anxiety, the chase. Why? Because that's what we're focused upon. Anxiety is fear-based. So the question becomes, can we have anxiety or can we fear money and simultaneously attract it? No, I don't think so!

If we're in a desperate search for a perfect relationship, coming from a position of trying to overcome our loneliness, what we get instead of a loving relationship is more loneliness. Why? Because that's our focus. What we pursue will always elude us. What we become we will attract into our lives. If we become the perfect mate, we will attract the perfect mate! On the other hand, if we become perfect loneliness, what we attract in return is more of the same. So, the answer is to let go of the loneliness, not to overcome or push it away.

Here are some of the most commonly asked questions regarding letting go:

QUESTION: How does letting go compare with other forms of self-improvement?

ANSWER: It doesn't really. Most self-improvement programs are intellectual. They are targeted toward changing one's mind through learning and applying a certain system or technique.

Letting go, on the other hand, is not trying to force

our minds into learning and applying a technique. In fact, letting go is not trying to force our minds to do anything at all. When we attempt to force our minds to do a certain thing, we are actually feeding the problem we are attempting to overcome. Self-improvement definitely works, but only to the degree that we can change our nonsupportive belief systems. And the only way to change an outdated belief is to first release the emotional energy keeping it alive in the first place. So self-improvement without letting go will result in an endless cycle of frustration going nowhere.

Letting go is really very simple. There is no system to follow. Letting go is as simple as observing our own nonresourcefulness as it arises, acknowledging it and saying, "Here I am doing it again." Then without buying into it, without self-judgment, return to the moment. In the beginning, we'll catch ourselves after the fact. We'll catch ourselves saying, "I can't believe I just did it again." After a while, with a little practice, we'll begin to catch ourselves in the middle of the act. We'll say, "Here I am again," right in the middle of being angry, or whatever. Then after a little more practice, we'll begin to catch ourselves before we get into it. The more we let go, the easier it becomes. Remember, the simple act of self-observation in itself is letting go.

QUESTION: What does "being in the moment" mean?

ANSWER: Being in the moment simply means this: "Wherever you are, be there!" If we are caught up in a past mistake, we can't be in the moment. Why? Because we are lost in the past. In one way we are in the moment, but what we are really doing is reliving a past experience in the moment. If we are worrying about our future, we can't truly be here. If we are cleaning the house, we should be right there with cleaning the house. We should observe the feelings we have that interrupt the work: "I don't like this." "The vacuum is noisy." "I shouldn't have to do this work, I have a college degree." If we are cutting the grass or driving the car or whatever, we should be right there, not hating what we're doing, but being with the job at hand. When we're in the moment, we become more efficient, more effective, and more resourceful and happy overall. We need to let go of all those extra thoughts and feelings that have absolutely nothing to do with the job at hand. If we hate our job, for example, we'll get caught up in the hate for our job and find ourselves closed to new possibilities and opportunities.

Do What You Do with Love

I remember my first job. I worked in a gas station. I believed that I was the best gas-station attendant in the whole world. I was really good, and I knew it. When a customer would come in, I would give them the best service that they had ever received anywhere. I would greet them with a smile, check their oil, check the air in their tires, wash their windshield, sweep out their car, etc. When I would bring back their change, I would thank them in a way that they had never been thanked before. One day after I had gone through the whole routine with a customer and brought back his change, as I walked away, he got out of the car and said, "Excuse me, young man, but could I ask you a question?" I said, "Sure." And he said, "What are doing working in this gas station?" I said, "Well, it's my job." "And you are very good at it," he said. "But you have a lot more on the ball than working in this station. You ought to be working in the factory." "The factory?" I said. "I could never qualify for that job." He explained that he was one of the supervisors, and that he could arrange for me to be hired, which he did.

After about a year of working in the factory, I became the number-one worker out of about 9,000 people. They rated us with an efficiency program, which included giving us a certain amount of time to do a certain job. I did the job of over four people. I could produce over thirty-two hours of work in eight hours. One day someone approached me and said, "Hey, Britt, what are you doing working in this factory? You've got more on the ball than working here. You should be in sales."

In less than a week I was a full-time salesman. I struggled for over a year and just couldn't make any money. In fact I ended up losing everything I owned trying to figure out how to sell. I refused to give up and as a result of my persistence a man from the company came by one day and showed me what I was doing wrong. Within six months I was the number-one salesperson in the company, selling two to three times what anyone else could sell.

A man who worked with me in my first job at the gas station (we'll call him Bill) was a habitual complainer. He complained about everything. When a customer would come in, he would complain, "It's too hot," "It's too cold," or "Don't they know that it's closing time," etc. Several times daily Bill, in his complaining way, would say, "One of these days I am getting out of here."

Twenty-five years later, I was back in that town. While I was there, I decided to stop by the gas station where I used to work. To my surprise, guess who I discovered still working there? Bill! After twenty-five years, he was still saying, "One day I'm going to get out of here." What do you think the odds are that someone will come by and ask Bill, "What are you doing working in this place? You've got a lot more on the ball than working here"?

Here's the moral to the story. If you do what you do with love, you'll eventually have only what you love in your life. This doesn't mean that we necessarily have to love what we do; what I'm saying is to do it with love, and there's a difference. Another way of saying it is, "be the best you can be at whatever you do." When we are being our best, we are doing it with love. When we are being our best, we are in a resourceful state, which leaves us wide open for new possibilities or opportunities.

When we become the best that we can be at whatever we are doing, the universe steps in and provides us with a better opportunity to become even better. I never even had a thought of leaving the gas-station job, but as soon as I had become the best gas-station attendant in the world (at least in my opinion), the universe went to work for me. Looking down, it said, "Well, there's Jim Britt working in that station, and his vision is simply to be the best he can be. It appears that he has reached his limits, so we'd better provide him with a better opportunity to further his growth." If we haven't discovered and learned all we can where we are currently, we don't get to move on to bigger and better things. That's the reason some feel stuck while others seem to be always moving on to better opportunities.

When you do what you do with love, you eventually have only what you love in your life.

If we observe our thoughts, feelings, emotions and behaviors drifting in any way from being the best we can be, simply let go and return to the present. This applies whether we're mowing the lawn, having a conversation with a friend or having dinner with the family. If we observe ourselves drifting away in any way, then return to the present. In other words, if we are at work, we should be working. If we are playing, we should play. If we are spending time with the family, we should be there with the family. If we are exercising, we should pay attention to what we are doing. Wherever you are, be there! That's what is meant by being in the moment.

QUESTION: What are feelings made of?

ANSWER: ENERGY! Everything in the universe is made of energy, wouldn't you agree? The computer I'm using, the clothes I'm wearing, the book you are reading and even our bodies are made of energy, the same energy. Everything is made of energy. The pen that I have in my pocket is made of energy. It is someone's idea of what to do with the usable energy. The pen is what you might call "trapped energy." In other words, it is already being used for some purpose. The plastic the pen is made of, even though it comes from a petroleum product, is not usable to fuel your car. Why? Because it is trapped in another form. All energy is both "expansive" and usable, or it is "restrictive" and already being used for some purpose. As an example, "I am lonely" is energy that is restricted, already being used for something. It is trapped energy and not usable for anything else as long as we are hanging on to it, using it for being lonely. On the other hand, "I feel loved" is a different use of the same energy. "I feel loved" is resourceful and expansive, and can be used to create anything we want in our lives.

Let's look at it in another way. Let's say that everything is made out of snow. And let's say that snow is energy, which it is. We pick up some snow and make a snowball. Now the snow is solid. It's more like a ball of ice, and we can throw it. It is no longer in its original form. If you spread it out, it becomes snow once again.

Another way to look at it is to turn water into ice by freezing it. The water is energy. The ice is trapped energy. Both are the same energy; only one is trapped in place, while the other is flowing. This is like "lonely" and "love." One is trapped in place, the other is flowing.

All the upsets we experience can only exist if we keep them trapped in place. When we let go, we neutralize the trapped energy, allowing it to flow once again. We turn the ice into flowing water, the loneliness into love.

QUESTION: Why can't we just love more? If we love more, won't these unwanted feelings eventually just go away?

ANSWER: I've heard it said many times that if we all just become more loving toward one another, everything would be just fine, as if being more loving can be done intentionally. We try to be more loving, then we fail. We then feel guilty and beat ourselves up because we can't love more. The next thing we do is to develop a nonresourceful attitude toward loving, thinking that we can't do it. The reason we can't be more loving is that we are going about it in the wrong way. We approach it through the mind, and the mind never produces love. No matter how hard we try to mentally convince ourselves to feel love, we can never succeed. By trying to mentally talk ourselves into being more loving, what we are really doing is setting ourselves up to fail, which will in turn cause us to feel more incapable of loving. Our love will merely be a creation of our mind, which has no basis for reality. Only by no longer being motivated by loneliness, only by letting it go, will we truly discover how to give and receive love.

When you begin to feel loneliness or any other non-resourceful emotion, simply observe it and release it, which will allow real love—the real you—to show through. Remember that pain is nothing more than a signal, a mental alarm clock, alerting us that it's time to let go. It's just restrictive energy coming up to be released. It's telling us that it's time to wake up. The pain is actually our greatest gift of self-love. Every crisis, every nonresourceful feeling or situation, is a perfectly planned opportunity for us to let go and move forward in our development.

And now the most asked question of all:

QUESTION: What exactly is fear?

ANSWER: Fear is also trapped energy—nothing more, nothing less. However, because we experience fear so often, let me explain it in a little more detail. It's good to know where fear comes from. Fear is the expectation of pain. Fear is the result of taking a nonresourceful experience from our past, projecting it into the future, anticipating it happening again and then experiencing it in the present once again. It's simply using our imagination to make up an experience of pain. Fear is never about the present. It's only about the future, based on the past. It only *appears* to be happening to us now. Whatever we allow into our minds is treated as though it is a present-moment experience. Therefore, anticipating pain is the very same thing as experiencing it.

When we begin to let go more often, we'll begin to understand that the past only exists for the purpose of utilizing the practical knowledge that we have gained over our lifetime. It's good to know not to walk out of a ten-story window, or to not walk in front of a moving truck. That's practical, wouldn't you agree? Never, ever, should we allow the past to become a source of pain in our lives. It should only exist as a source of experience.

Our fears can take on the form of our constantly analyzing everything. When we overanalyze, we are creating a cover-up that's supposed to keep us safe in our own make-believe world. We fear letting go because we are afraid that we won't know who we are if we do. We think that when we let go we'll be totally out of control, when actually the opposite is true.

Often we need to let go in order to find out what we really need to let go of. In other words, we may need to let go of our fear in a relationship in order to realize that the real issue is not the fear but rather commitment. We may need to let go of the fear of losing our job to find out that our own self-doubt is the real issue. Anything we cling to will eventually cause us pain. When we cling to our fears, we have trapped the energy and given it a name: fear. As long as we hang on to it, it will cause us pain. Why? Because fear is trapped pain that can be used for nothing else until we let it go. When we let fear go, it becomes the flowing energy of love once again. God has granted us the ability to create anything we want out of love energy. Even fear is based in love. It starts with love, becomes fear when we make a choice to trap it, and then becomes love once again when we make a choice to let it go. Fear provides absolute proof that we as humans have the ability to create!

If fear is the expectation of pain, then its opposite must be the anticipation of pleasure. So when we let go of our fears, we can shift our focus to what we want, instead of what we don't want. We'll want to release our fear before turning our focus to something resourceful. If we have to struggle to shift our focus, the struggle can actually feed the fear. The only way fears can have any power over us is when we identify with them. For example, thinking that we are eight feet tall will have no effect on us at all, because we don't identify with being eight feet tall. We know that it's not us, so there's nothing to hang on to. On the other hand, if we think, "I am lonely," that has a hook, an emotional link to a previous experience. When we have a hook we begin to identify once again with the pain from our past, and we do it in the present moment.

When we identify with something, it becomes like glue: it "sticks" to us. If we challenge our fears through self-observation instead of becoming identified with them, they will lose their hold on us, or better yet, we will lose our hold on them.

The more we ask ourselves, "Where does this fear come from?" soon we'll find our fears appearing less and less often, with longer and longer space between them. We'll also discover that the space between our fears is who we really are. The more we let go of our fears, the greater the space between them grows.

So when do you do it? When do you let go? Do you set aside time to practice, or do you have to go away to practice it? Here's when you practice letting go: you practice it all the time. You practice it every waking moment of your life.

When you are in a traffic jam.

When you are in a meeting.

When you are having a meal.

When you are disciplining your children.

When you are in an argument with someone.

When you are stressed.

When you are stuck and don't know what to do next.

When you meet someone new.

When you can't sleep.

When you need answers.

When you feel nervous or anxious.

When you are worried.

You practice letting go any time a nonresourceful feeling is moving you further away from what you want in your life, further away from love.

High Action and Low Attachment

Letting go is about taking action from a position of resourcefulness rather than nonresourcefulness. Letting go is about high action and low attachment. Letting go lets us take solution-oriented action instead of problem-oriented action.

We should also avoid the temptation to be hard on ourselves for feeling nonresourceful. Getting rid of outdated habit patterns and emotions should be guiltless. Look at nonresourceful feelings not as your enemy but rather as an ally that's providing you with a wonderful opportunity for growth.

Any time we hear that familiar voice inside describing us, if it's not speaking with love and compassion, simply say, "That's how I used to be, that's not me now." You see, being open to a new way requires being able to view the old, not with anger or resentment, but rather with love and compassion. We should never let our past dictate how we live our present. We should just do the best we can and not concern ourselves over whether it was good enough. Just remember that every present moment is always brand-new. What happened to us in the past is not happening to us now, unless we allow it to.

In addition to the basics needed to sustain life—food, clothing, shelter, water, sunlight and oxygen—there is one other element most of us completely overlook, and that's love. We need love in order to survive. Any nonlove feeling actually threatens our very existence, just the same as not having oxygen would. Carrying around self-hate or nonlove feelings is simply a slower way to die. Every time we let go of a nonlove feeling, what we are really doing is changing cells and rebalancing the brain. The more you let go, the more the real you begins to appear—the one who's full of joy, happiness, self-confidence and peace of mind.

Starting today, allow every unplanned experience, every unexpected mishap, every nonresourceful thought, every unwanted feeling and emotion—no matter what it is or how much it hurts—to have a life of its own, to come up, to be released and to become free-flowing energy once again. Begin today to view your life with this higher understanding, an understanding that everything under the Sun, from emotions and thoughts, to thunder and lightning, has its own birth, life and death. The only reason that any part of our painful past exists at all is because we refuse to let it die its own natural death by letting it go.

Living with pain and disappointment is not a requirement. Letting go of what no longer supports us is not a requirement; it's simply a way of ending pain and disappointment in our lives.

3

Happiness Is Our Natural State

*True happiness
is
freedom
from everything
that
makes
you
unhappy*

Happiness. Everyone wants it. Everyone works toward it. The American dream ... health, wealth and the pursuit of happiness.

Happiness is defined as "the feeling of pleasure or contentment." What would make you happy? What would give you pleasure and contentment? Think about it for a moment. What would it really take to make you happy? How about having lots of money? Would that do it for you? Would that really make you happy? How about having a loving relationship? Would that do it for you? What about less stress, a more fulfilling career? What really stands in your way of having all the happiness you want?

Why do you think we're all so obsessed with being happy? We seek happiness because it's our natural state. You might say that we are "homesick." Happiness is a goal with which we were all born. However, there are inappropriate ways of achieving that goal. Pursuing happiness through bodily desires such as sex, for example, doesn't work because it builds dependence. This is not to suggest that we should not have or not want sex. However, if we use it as a means to find happiness, we will fall far short of our goal.

If we attempt to find happiness as a result of gaining acceptance from others, in material possessions or in having money, we will again be falling short of the happiness that is within our power to experience. All these methods are tied to external conditions, over which we have no control whatsoever, and therefore can never lead us to true, lasting happiness.

Unfortunately, most of the emphasis these days is on learning how to more effectively get what we think we need to be happy. What we are attempting to do, however, is satisfy our addictions. What we really need to do instead is to learn how to eliminate our addictions. We will always have activities, money, relationships and possessions, but instead of viewing them as sources of our happiness, they become expressions of our happiness.

When we begin to realize that nothing from the outside can help us find happiness, we are then free from the underlying sense of lack we all seem to have in our lives. When we lack nothing, we feel complete as we are. Feeling complete, we can then enter into a state of resourcefulness. Being resourceful leaves us open to attract fortunate circumstances. In other words, when we don't feel that we lack anything, we are open to receive. When we are in a state of lack, our focus is on our lack—thereby not leaving us open to receive new opportunities or resourceful solutions. When we're resourceful we can easily acquire material possessions, but we don't become dependent upon them for our happiness, and we never fear losing them, or our happiness. When we fear losing what we have—our money, relationship, etc.—the fear itself will cause us unhappiness. The key to happiness is to let go of our fears, to be happy with what we have, while creating what we want. Fear immobilizes. When we are experiencing fear we are stuck in the past or future where happiness does not and cannot exist.

We've Become Attached to Our Circumstances

You may be asking yourself, if I don't find happiness outside myself in what I accomplish and what I have, then where do I find it?

Often we are told to seek happiness within, and not much more is said. The meaning is very unclear. "Seek happiness within" is misleading and can be a trap in itself. So we decide that if happiness is not from a material source, then it must be from a nonmaterial source, such as our own concept of God, a guru, or some leader or spiritual teacher. With all this in mind, we continue to be aggressive in our pursuit of happiness, and we stay attached to our outdated idea of how or where happiness is found.

There's a story about the fishermen in one of the old countries. Every morning they would go out early and fish until midafternoon. They would then come in and unload their catch on the dock, spending the rest of the afternoon preparing their boat for the next day's fishing. Their wives, while the men were getting the boat ready, would put the day's catch in their baskets, place the baskets on their heads and go to the market. One day they had to go to a market that was further away, requiring an overnight stay. As it began to get dark, the women started to look for a comfortable place to bed down for the night. One woman spotted a beautiful meadow full of wildflowers and suggested they sleep there. They laid their baskets of fish at the edge of the meadow and walked out among the beautiful flowers and the wonderful fragrance, and bedded down for the night. They tossed and turned for hours but they just couldn't go to sleep. Finally, one woman picked up her blanket and walked to the edge of the field where the baskets of fish were sitting. She laid her head down beside the basket of stinking fish, and within seconds she fell fast asleep.

The moral to the story is that sometimes we get so attached to our stinking circumstances and old beliefs that we can't feel comfortable amid the beauty that surrounds us. Another way of saying it is that we become so attached to our self-imposed limitations that we are not open to a better way. We have literally become hypnotized by our own inner dialog. We create a beautiful vision of how we want our lives to be and then we hear that familiar whisper, "Don't forget your self-judgment report card. You don't deserve to have that. You can't be happy without this or that." We have become hypnotized by our own limited beliefs.

So how do we break this hypnotic spell?

The very first step is to get clear about what we really want in our lives. The second is to take responsibility for our feelings. That's not responsibility for how we feel or how we came to feel that way, but rather to take responsibility for changing what we feel, if needed. Taking responsibility for what we feel can put us back into a self-judgment pattern once again, but taking responsibility for changing how we feel is the very first step toward letting go, which enables self-growth.

If we want our circumstances to change, we have to make a conscious choice to change the rules, because circumstances won't change until we change.

Here are four important points to consider:

1. If you want to achieve a different result in your life, you must do something different.
2. In order to do something different, you must first know something different to do.
3. In order to know something different to do, you must at least suspect that, if the key to being happy were in the places you'd been looking, you would have found it by now.
4. You must be open to trying a new way. If you want to make a change, you must be open to changing the rules of your game.

We Can Change the Rules

Let's say that you and I sit down to play a game of checkers. We each have twelve pieces—twelve are red and twelve are black. We both know that the objective is to jump all our opponent's pieces as we move across the board in one direction. When either of us reaches the other side safely, we are crowned. Now we have a new advantage. We can move freely in either direction. The game continues until one of us has lost all our pieces.

Now what if I step in and change the rules? What if I crowned all my pieces up front, so that I could move in either direction from the start? I would have an unfair advantage over you, wouldn't I? Or maybe I went a little further in changing the rules and took my hand and just wiped all of your pieces off the board and said, "I won!" Now, you might say, "You can't do that, there are rules." And I say, "Well, I changed the rules." You say, "You can't change the rules." "Why not? Who wrote the rules? Why can't I change them? Who says I can't?"

We probably wouldn't want to play checkers that way. It wouldn't be a lot of fun for either of us, would it?

What about the game of life? What about your own happiness? Who wrote the rules? Why can't we change them? Who says we can't?

Let's look at the game of chess. We have the same board as for checkers and a few more pieces. How many moves can we make? How many choices do we have? Virtually unlimited! Same playing field and a few more pieces than with checkers, but we have almost unlimited choices.

The same principle applies to the game of life. We all play on the same playing field, and we have truly unlimited choices. Every single choice we make creates a different future. The question is, are we making intelligent choices or choices from convenience? Are we simply going along with the rules that someone else may have set up for us or that we have set up for ourselves by our own limiting beliefs?

Until we make the intelligent choice to do life differently, we'll continue to play within our old rules with a limited number of choices and a limited amount of happiness.

About seventeen years ago, I was living the "good life," with all the trappings of what you might consider success. I woke early one morning to a beautiful sunrise looking out over a beautiful view of the countryside. I began to think about my life. As I contemplated, I thought of how I used to tell my former wife, "One day when we have it all—money, house, etc.—then we are going to be happy." Then it hit me—I was alone. My former wife and my two children were no longer with me. They lived in another part of the country. My marriage had ended in divorce. I had it all, but I was living alone. I had said I was doing it for them, and now they were gone.

A question suddenly crossed my mind: "If I'm so happy, how come I'm hurting so much inside?"

Right then, that day, that moment, I made a choice to

change the rules. I made a conscious choice to change the rules regarding my concept of happiness.

Where to Find Happiness

What is happiness anyway?

I first looked at what I thought happiness wasn't. These thoughts crossed my mind. *Happiness is not being broke.* That wouldn't be happiness, would it?

Happiness is not having a broken relationship. That's not happiness.

Happiness is not being lonely. And my list went on.

Happiness is not driving a junk car.

Happiness is not living where you don't want to live.

Happiness is not being sick.

Happiness is not working in a profession you hate.

I thought, *None of these things would be happiness, would they?*

I set out to find out what would be the ultimate happiness. So I took the same questions and turned them around.

If I just had money, would that do it, would that be the ultimate happiness?

If I just had the perfect relationship?

Not being lonely, would that do it for me?

*If I could just get that new car that I really want? Would that
really make me happy?*

What about the perfect profession?

If I could just get my life organized, would that do it?

If I could just get away for a while?

Then it hit me like a ton of bricks. If having those
things—money, cars, etc.—was not happiness, and *not* having
those things was not happiness, then what or where could
one find happiness?

I suddenly realized that happiness only happened in the
moment. Happiness couldn't happen yesterday, nor could it
happen tomorrow. Now is the only place that happiness can
ever exist. So I concluded that if happiness only happens in
the moment, then *all* those things had to be happiness.
Happiness is whatever's happening right here, right now!
What else could it be?

So, happiness is being lonely.

Happiness is having a fulfilling relationship.

Happiness is being sick.

Happiness is being healthy.

Happiness is being broke.

Happiness is having money.

Happiness has to be whatever we are going through right
now. We are not our past or our future. We have only become
temporarily identified with it. Once we are aware of this,

who we thought we were or what we thought we had to have or become is over! The only time is now. There is no past or future.

Many people believe they are living in the moment, but in reality they are fearfully running from one moment to the next trying to find happiness. We very often fear what we don't truly understand. By living in the present, we begin to realize that our fears are simply mental mistakes or misguided rumors. We can begin to see them for what they really are. We'll begin to see that our fears are simply a gift presented to us as a perfectly planned opportunity to let go and grow.

It's interesting how the words *happiness* and *happening* are so similar. Happiness is whatever's happening at any given moment.

At any moment there is just what's happening. That's it! Nothing more!

If we tie our happiness to some external condition somewhere in the future, it becomes impossible to ever find happiness. Why? Because there is no future, just like there is no past. The only reality is what's happening right here, right now, in this moment. NOW is what's happening. NOW is reality. Trying to find happiness out there in the future somewhere is just as much of an impossibility as trying to find happiness by reliving our past.

So often we become caught up in the illusion of it all. We say, "Forget reality, I want more! More is what would make me happy. I can't be happy with what I have, I need more to really be happy." Having more is great. I believe we should all have more of the finer things in life, but having more should be the *result* of our happiness, not the *cause* of it.

This very moment is it! It's all there is: nothing more and nothing less. You may be asking yourself, "How can I be in the moment when I have bills to pay or an important meeting next week?"

Here's the real question. Which would be more effective, to be focused in the moment, on the here and now, or on the future that doesn't yet exist? I'm not saying do not plan for the future. What I am saying is that we should make our plans for the future, and then stay focused in the moment where the real action is, where reality exists.

Every moment, if we're truly in it, offers a wealth of opportunities. When we are truly in the moment, we can see the conflict between what we want, how we think things should be and what is really happening. In other words, when we're in the moment we are open to receiving solutions and seeing opportunities as they are presented to us. We become solution-oriented rather than problem-oriented.

Logic tells us to look at life this way:
When I get through all these problems,
Right after the first of the year,
As soon as my money problems get better,
As soon as the kids are older,
Then I'll relax and be happy and live in the moment.

Well it ain't gonna happen! Why? Because all our stuff, all our problems—the house payment, the kids, etc.—that's our life.

A good friend of mine used to say, "If you're alive and you don't have problems, you've got problems." That's what life is about, solving problems. The problem is that we're not happy. The problem is, I need to make more money. The problem is I am lonely. The problem list goes on and on.

I heard a great line in a movie a while back. The man was lying on his deathbed as he said to his friend at his bedside, "All I ever wanted to do was live a normal life." His friend responded by saying, "There is no normal life, there's only life." There are always going to be problems to deal with—family problems, relationship problems, business problems, money problems and personal problems. That's what life is all about, solving problems. That's how we discover more of what we are. That's how we grow.

There Is No Stress in the Moment

If we're alive and we don't have things to deal with—people problems, bills, kids, etc.—then we're probably not alive at all, we're probably dreaming the whole thing. Problems and stuff are a part of life. When we get through all that we're dealing with right now, we'll simply be through all that we're dealing with, and that's it! Then there will be more to follow. We'll have a whole new set of reasons to not be happy and not live in the moment. A friend of mine told me one day that she was going on a retreat for two months of silence so that she could find herself, to discover the truth of who she is. When I saw her a few months later after she'd returned, I asked her about her silent-retreat adventure. Her response was, "Interesting. It was interesting." She said she thought she would have to go again in order to get the full effect.

We don't have to look "out there" to figure out anything about who we are. There's nothing to figure out. There's nothing to acquire. You don't have to go off to a retreat or anywhere else to find the truth. On the other hand, if going to a retreat, attending a seminar, reading a book or whatever can help you learn how to see the truth, it can be a very beneficial tool. A seminar cannot teach truth. Only you can discover the truth. There is no path to the truth except your own.

Any aid is a good aid. If reading a book can help you in some way discover your truth, then read it.

The stresses we face today will always seem insurmountable if we continue to look at them through the eyes of the past. There is no stress in the moment. Why? Because stress is created from fear. Fear is where the past and the future meet the here and now. There is no fear in the moment, unless we bring it into the moment from the past or the future.

Emotional stress is the net effect of a condition you are resisting or trying to escape, but the condition has no power in itself. Nothing outside has the power to create stress. For example, for one person the loss of a job may be a painful experience if it is not wanted, while for another the same experience may mean freedom.

You can always choose to get a prescription to control your stress, but all of us know that is not the real answer. Expanding our consciousness to see the truth of our stress is the only permanent solution.

The fact is that we can only wake up and see the truth right here, right now. There is no need to go through a painful quest. We are exactly where we need to be. The feast is spread before us. All we need to do is eat!

Whether we see our lives as an opportunity or a burden depends on our point of view, not our circumstances. We would like to believe, as many do, that our external circumstances are the cause of what we're experiencing. However, all we can *truly* experience is ourselves. How do we feel, how do we perceive life and how do we react in a given situation? We attempt to avoid our unpleasant feelings by staying focused on our past mistakes and worrying about future events, not realizing that our focus on the past and the future is what's causing us to feel that way in the first place.

Our objective should be to simply see what the truth of the problem is and deal with it. The faster we deal with it, the sooner it will go away. It's called living consciously—not for the sake of a belief or an idea—but for the sake of living in the moment where the action is, in our authentic power, without resistance. Once we truly observe and begin to see, we begin to live our lives more consciously. We begin to see the real truth.

We expend most of our creativity, imagination and vital energy living in the past or the future so that we can avoid the present, which consists of real life.

Happiness, resourcefulness, creativity, peace of mind, love and living stress-free all take place in the moment. Any time we are out of the moment, we are avoiding those things.

Living in the moment is a condition worth striving for. Why? Because our lives are taking place in the moment. When we get caught up with expectations of the future, which are almost always based on past experiences of lack, we cannot experience life as it is, which is right here, right now. We never grow or experience any degree of happiness by daydreaming about a future full of wonderful events, or by remembering and getting caught up in our past accomplishments or mistakes.

The process of setting goals simply for the purpose of having more things becomes like a roller-coaster ride. We anticipate the ride and the thrill of it all. Then we get on board and enjoy the ride. Up, down, around and upside down, it's definitely thrilling. After the ride is over, we get off at the same place where we began, ready for a new ride, which will eventually bring us back to the same place once again.

I'm by no means saying that we shouldn't achieve things or have goals. Being achievement-oriented is part of being human. But in order to experience happiness and personal growth, we must experience life as it is, in this moment. Growth comes from our experiences of anger, sadness, fear and anxiety. Our challenges can be our best teachers, and they are often our only teachers when it comes to our own growth. Our fears and anger are truly our greatest gifts because they offer us an opportunity to let them go and to move past them. When we attempt to escape from what life hands us by avoiding our feelings, we do not grow. Getting everything we want in the world won't protect us from being unhappy, because it could all be gone tomorrow, or even today.

Happiness Comes *from* Us, Not *at* Us

There are various levels of unhappiness, but ignorance is number one. We ignore our happiness. The real keys to happiness are clarity, self-observation and letting go of all that does not support our happiness. If we focus attention on the present, we can always make it better. When we improve upon the present, what comes later will also improve. Self-awareness is not enough. Most of us are aware that we are caught on this emotional treadmill. Getting clear about what we want—self-observation, which is simply backing off and taking a higher view—is the answer, because with a higher view, we can then see what we need to let go of in order to become happy.

Our feelings, good or bad, resourceful or not, are not the master of our lives, they are only experiences, nothing more, nothing less, just experiences. We are the masters of our lives, and our happiness will be followed by our own self-discovery of what we really are. Our happiness comes *from* us, not *at* us. The results we produce, or what we have in our lives, should make no difference in maintaining our level of happiness. The key is to treat our results, good or not so good, with indifference. An outcome is an outcome, not good or bad, simply an outcome. Why can't we just be good rather than bad? The reason is that it is impossible to establish good or bad. They aren't absolutes. Good or bad are only judgments or beliefs. They are merely perceptions based on our ignorance of what's really happening.

We see a man steal a loaf of bread and say he was bad for doing so. We then discover he took the bread to feed his starving children. Was the act good or bad? It depends on our perspective—what we believe to be good or what we believe to be bad. Good or bad is not the issue. It's how we deal with the event that's the real issue. It's how we let it affect us. It's observing the truth in the moment.

During some wars, both sides claim to have God on their side. It is very clear to each side that they are doing good. Both claim to be good, and both claim the other to be bad.

Again, good or bad is not the issue. It's only through seeing reality that we can even hope to find what lies beyond our ideas of good and bad.

Emotional excitement is not being happy, either. It is artificial and eventually crashes. True happiness is total freedom from anything that makes you unhappy.

As an example, if we were hurt at some point in our past, until we let go of that past hurt we have no space for happiness. We all hold an attachment to the past in some way. This is a characteristic of the human ego. We see the past as somehow sacred. We fantasize about events gone by long ago. We hang on to the memories of our failings, to loved ones who have passed on, etc. These sorts of attitudes are nonresourceful and will keep us from living our true potential in the moment. They will keep us separated from love, from happiness and from taking advantage of the gift of our authentic power. How could we possibly remain connected to our power when we are preoccupied with feelings and memories from the past?

If we are to ever find happiness, we must learn to concentrate on not reacting to the buttons that we have allowed to be pushed in our minds and hearts all these years. Did someone in your past disappoint you? Did someone cause you pain? Did you fail in a business deal? Whatever it is, if you want to experience more love, find happiness or stay tapped into your authentic power, you must, on a daily basis, let go of your emotional attachment to these issues. You must learn to see the truth within yourself regarding how you have been treating these anxieties. Just remember, the past is gone, the future doesn't exist, and peace and happiness are our natural state. It only happens in this moment.

The present moment is perfect freedom. It is where unhappiness does not exist.

We all attempt to "master" our negative feelings, thinking that will make us happy. A master can be defined as, "That part of us who existed prior to any outside influence, and that will still exist underneath all the layers of outside influence, which we have allowed to become a part of us." Spending all our time fantasizing about a perfect future simply wastes our precious opportunities for a perfect now. You cannot master negative feelings, but you can let them go and move past them.

Our life is really about perfect moments, isn't it? We don't remember our lives in the past, but rather we remember the moments we've experienced. What if you captured one of your life's most precious moments? What would the memory of that moment hold for you?

Think of a perfect moment you've experienced. Can you remember what happened before or following that moment? The reason we remember the moment is that we were in it. We truly lived that moment!

Right now you are experiencing one of those moments. What memory will this moment hold for you? Are you truly in this moment or somewhere lost in the past or the future?

Live This Moment

I called a friend of mine one day. His assistant said that he had gone to his mountain cabin to get away for a few days. The next day I called him at his cabin and asked him if he was enjoying his time away. He said that he was spending all his time thinking about problems at the office. I asked him to do himself a favor and take a walk on his property, and during his walk I wanted him to think about nothing else except his walk. He called me back a while later and shared with me what he had seen. He said he saw things that he never knew were there. He saw ants, beaver, elk, an eagle and some springs bubbling up out of the ground. He was amazed at all he saw simply by being in the moment.

Take fifteen minutes—right now, if possible—and take a walk. Put all your attention on experiencing the moment and see what happens. Do that every day; you'll be pleasantly surprised by the results.

Just stop and notice once in a while how we spend our whole lives trying to arrive at some destination. Where is it we think we are going? What is it that we feel needs to be accomplished? All the pursuit of learning and personal growth is simply for the purpose of understanding that we already have everything and that there is nothing to get. It is our own perception of who we think we are that believes something must be missing. In reality, everything is perfect just the way it is. Our pain and suffering come from one source, and that is our own resistance to our happiness, which is our natural state. Pain and suffering result when we don't allow life to flow without resistance, as it should. Stress and hardship occur when we don't accept our fear as a gift that hastens our own growth. All our pain comes from the lack of being present with ourselves, and from the belief that we need something more to be happy.

Trusting that everything is unfolding perfectly for the purpose of enhancing our own growth is the key.

You may think that this approach to life is a bit different, or even strange. Most people don't want to believe that life can be that simple. They want to believe that it has to be more difficult, that there needs to be some kind of system, or guru to follow, in order to be happy. By following a system we only become a slave to the system, and we are limited by it as well. We become trapped and limited by the system. When we're trapped by anything at all, we are no longer free to experience all the happiness available to us.

We've been conditioned to complicate everything, to look for answers outside ourselves, to find someone to offer us a system to follow. We want someone to feed us the answers to living a happy life. Personal development is not what we need. What we need instead is waking up. If we wake up to the fact that every moment of our life is our teacher, we cannot avoid growing. If we truly understand that every moment of our life is all we have, we cannot avoid growing. If we are truly living in each moment, we need no outside authority to show us the way to live.

Let Go of Yesterday and Tomorrow

So, what is happiness? It is living fully in the moment with no attachments to yesterday or tomorrow. We already do this to one degree or another. Think about it. All that we have accomplished in our life is a result of the time we spent living in the moment where the action is. All the memories we have, all the things we have and all that we have learned . . . all happened in the moment sometime in our past. As I have said before, but it's worth repeating, a lot of people think they are living in the moment, when in reality they are running from one moment to the next.

It takes courage to let go and forgive the past so that we can give our full attention to the task at hand. When we are eating, we should be with our meal. We should concentrate on eating. When we are working we should concentrate on our work. If we are exercising, we should be with the experience of exercising. If we are with our family or those we love, why not concentrate on being right there with them? Our lives are happening right now! Everything else is just a thought about the past or the future. We are not our past; we have only become unconsciously identified with it in the present. Allowing the natural flow of a nonresourceful feeling from beginning to end will free us from identifying with it.

If we are in a conversation with someone, we should concentrate on being right there instead of letting our thoughts or our imagination carry us away to someplace else. Wouldn't that be a more effective way to live? When we are making love, doesn't it make more sense to be right there? When we begin to live more fully in the moment, without attachment to the past or the future, we'll begin to see more beauty in our lives. We'll accomplish more in less time. We'll begin to discover a sense of freedom that we've never experienced before. Life will become one continuous celebration. Celebration only happens in the moment. Celebration produces joy. Look for the joy in every moment. Look for a reason to celebrate every moment. Joy travels from the inside outward, then it returns again, and it only operates in the present. There is no joy in the past or the future, only in the now.

We are already in reality, whether we see it or not. Reality is whatever's happening this very moment. We are never separated from reality. Reality is not out there or around the next corner or anywhere except right here.

Most of us have been taught that we have to figure something out in order for our lives to work, and that conditioning is exactly why our lives aren't working the way we wish they would. The reality is that all we need to figure out is what's going on right now and remain in that moment.

Look for the Joy in Every Moment

Having feelings of unhappiness is not a requirement. Letting go of nonsupportive feelings and emotions is not a requirement, and living in the moment is not a requirement: they are simply methods of ending unhappiness.

We cannot make a wrong decision about our future, because a present decision does not create a future event. Present decisions create present events. On the other hand a present experience that we hang on to can and will create a result in a moment somewhere in the future.

A decision does not make the future turn out a certain way. It's how we continue to think, feel, speak and act that makes the future turn out the way it does.

So what does it really mean to stay focused on the present? It means to become more intimately and consciously aware of the input from your senses, to become more fully observant of what's really going on in your world, inside as well as outside. Begin to pay attention to how you think and feel. Begin to observe the words you speak and the actions you take.

Someone once said it like this:

Yesterday is history;
tomorrow is a mystery.
Today is a gift;
that's why it is called the present.

When you can be happiness, you can find happiness. Forget the left-brain programming you've learned from society. Shut out the logic and reason that tells you to keep bringing up the past in order to protect you from being hurt again. Instead you should hook yourself up to your intuition, hook yourself up to this moment. Use all your senses. Begin today to be happy. Smell happiness, taste it, see it, feel it and think it. Just be every possible image of happiness.

My three-year-old son Walker said it best. Just before Christmas, he woke up one morning and awakened me telling me that this day was going to be the happiest day of his life. I asked him why that was. He said that today was the day that he was going to get to buy gifts for everyone he loved. He wasn't thinking about tomorrow or yesterday, only the happiness that he was experiencing now.

Remember that happiness only happens in this moment, so you shouldn't let the magnetic pull of your past or future dictate how you live your life in the present. If you begin to pay close attention to the present, you can always improve upon it. If you improve upon the present, what comes later will also be better. Plan for the future, let go of the past and live in the moment where the action is, where happiness and love are always present.

4

Self-Observation

Self-observation
allows you
to clearly understand
what you
are seeing
rather
than being
controlled by it

A number of years ago, a woman approached me following a lecture I presented before a convention of corporate executives and their spouses. She said she had heard a lot about letting go, and wanted to know if I could spend some time with her. She said she was experiencing some conflicts in her life that she hadn't been able to resolve. She asked me if she attended my seminar could I give her a system that would transform her life? My immediate response was, "No, my seminar will not transform your life. There is no system that I know of that can transform your life." She said, "But I thought you offered a system for people to follow that will lead to personal transformation?" My response was, "No, I only present ideas that have worked in my own life. As far as transformation, that's your choice. It's up to you what you do with the information."

It's up to each of us what direction we take and what information we choose to utilize for our own transformation. Transformation begins with self-awareness. The definition of *awareness* is "having knowledge or realization of." In other words, to experience transformation, we must become aware of the fact that transformation is needed in the first place.

There's a story about a man who was well-schooled as an entrepreneur and businessperson. One morning he was out for a drive along a deserted country road when his attention was drawn toward some sort of activity in the middle of a field under a huge apple tree. As he drew closer, he noticed a farmer running around under the tree. As he drove even closer he saw that the farmer was running around under the tree chasing about two hundred little pigs. When he caught one, he would hold it up to the tree and let the pig eat an apple off the tree. He would then put the pig down and begin chasing another, which he would hold up to the tree to eat an apple. He continued the same process over and over for more than an hour.

The passerby, being well-schooled as a creative entrepreneur, thought there must surely be a better, more efficient method. So he decided to have a chat with the farmer. He approached the farmer and said, "Excuse me, sir. I've been watching you for about an hour now, and would you mind telling me what you are doing?" The farmer responded by saying, "Well, I'm feeding these apples to my pigs. They like apples." The man looked at him, perplexed, and said, "Why don't you just pick all the apples off the tree, throw them on the ground, and let the pigs run around and eat the apples? Wouldn't that save a lot of time?" And the farmer responded, "What's time to a pig?"

Do you think there might be a better way? There may be one from your perspective, but how about from the farmer's perspective? Probably not, or he would be using it.

Our Beliefs Are What Limit Us

In order to attain a different result, we have to do something different. In order to *do* something different, we must first *know* something different. And in order to know something different we must first suspect that our present method of operation needs improving. That's called awareness. There is no system I could offer to change anyone's perceptions unless they thought their perceptions needed improving and were open to a new and better way.

We may offer ideas, but people have to take the initiative and observe their own methods—their actions and beliefs—and even then only they can make the choice to change their methods.

If I believe a certain thing to be true, or if I believe that my way is the only way, then I will be heavily invested in protecting my belief. But on the other hand, if something or someone wakes me up to the truth or to a better way, and I discover that I have a choice, I then free myself to look with a new perspective.

Our beliefs hold us back. For example, you may be experiencing being broke. You say, "I am broke." Or you may possess a certain degree from college, perhaps in psychology; so you say, "I am a psychologist." Or you may say, "I resent successful people"; therefore, "I am resentful."

Our beliefs have become so imprinted on our identity that we have built powerful support systems to reassure one another that what we do and what we have is who we are.

Intention is the starting point for change. In order to make a permanent change, we must first have the intention to understand ourselves. Self-knowledge is the beginning of wisdom and transformation. Self-knowledge cannot be given to us by learning a system or from someone else. Each individual must discover it for himself or herself. If our intention to know ourselves is weak, then just a casual wish or hope to change is of very little significance.

We seem to always want to change outside circumstances, change other people, change the government, change our relationship, change our job and so on in an attempt to change our lives.

All transformation begins with self-knowledge. Without knowing who we are, there is no foundation for correct thinking. There is no reality. Without a foundation for correct thinking based upon self-knowledge, there can be no transformation.

Reality is the starting point. Have you ever heard the statement "the truth will set you free"? The truth begins with an undistorted understanding of what we are. That's what the statement means. It is not referring to merely telling the truth, although that's a good place to start, but rather to understanding or seeing the truth. That's where transformation begins. In fact that's the only place it can begin. Reality is essential. Reality gives us true freedom. Reality comes from the understanding of what is, whereas when we're working toward reality through some system that someone else has created for us to follow, that's called postponement. It's the cover-up of what we would like it to be.

In order to create a new structure for our lives and to let go of the old one, we must first and foremost truly want to be free. To be free, we must want to know reality. Without knowing reality, there is no freedom. Without freedom, there can be no transformation. We must be willing to look at what is, not just how we would like it to be.

The real difficulty most of us incur results from not knowing ourselves. Out of frustration, we set out to find a system to follow as a means of becoming better and having more. We want a system that will guarantee our transformation.

No one can invent a system for self-transformation. By following a system of any kind, we will merely produce a result that is created by the system itself, which will always be limited, and the result of a system will obviously not be self-understanding. How could it possibly be since all systems are by their very nature limited?

Say you decide to follow a system of using affirmations as a method of transforming your life. While affirmations may change your mind temporarily or even in some cases permanently, they won't provide you a method for seeing truth. Seeing truth is the only way to transformation, and you can only know the truth when you see it. No one can teach it to you by teaching you a system. On the other hand the system may provide you with some tool to help you see your truth.

If we live our lives according to some preset pattern, we can't be reality-based, because a set pattern does not lead to self-understanding. If God had meant for us to follow a set system, he would not have created unique individuals. God would have cut only one pattern for the entire human race, or given us a set system to follow. There is no system to follow for transformation. On the other hand if a system causes us to look at ourselves, then there is value in it. Any system that does not cause us to look at ourselves is at best incomplete.

Everyone is searching for the correct path to truth. But the real truth is that there is no correct path, except the one we create for ourselves. The only method I know for gaining truth is through self-observation.

Truth simply means seeing versus not seeing. It means being in touch with what's going on around us as opposed to having our view clouded by our own beliefs and thoughts, or the beliefs and thoughts of others.

I heard that if you drop a frog into boiling water, he'd immediately jump out. But if you place a frog in lukewarm water then gradually raise the temperature to the boiling point he will stay there until he dies.

Unlike a frog, we have the capacity to see when we are slipping too far into hot water, into an unhealthy situation. We can stop, observe the situation, and decide if we want to proceed or to take a different, more productive direction. We can only do this, however, if we are willing to see the reality of the situation, then act on what we know to be truth.

We can see truth only when we determine to see our situation for what it is. No one can learn the truth from another. If we do not have the resolve to see the truth, to see reality, there is certainly nothing any teacher can do for us.

Imagine that you are driving your car down the road at a high speed, and suddenly you see another car in your lane coming directly at you. A head-on collision is about to happen in about three seconds if you don't act fast. Are you going to take the time and weigh the pros and cons of continuing on your collision course? Of course not! If you are faced with a head-on collision, you're not going to contemplate the situation; you are going to act. You have no other choice, do you? You see the truth. You see reality!

Seeing truth is not being caught by any one particular view. It's not being a prisoner of your own or someone else's beliefs. Seeing truth is seeing what is actually happening at that moment.

We can want transformation. We can want to know the truth. We can want to gain greater wisdom. We can have the intention to have all these things, but none of them are possible without self-observation and letting go.

Whenever we experience any sort of problem or upset, we have simply come face to face with our own life level. Letting go of the pain of the upset is the only way we can move past our current life level. It takes courage to observe what happened to us in our past and to choose to no longer react to the pain. We will always suffer unconsciously what we do not face consciously. So when a problem or pain arises, ask not "what do I do now," but rather, "what do I need to understand?" Whether we see life as a hardship or an opportunity depends on our view, not our circumstances.

Self-observation is where we remain conscious of what we're thinking, feeling, speaking and acting. When we observe ourselves feeling fearful, if we really step back and observe, we'll begin to see the reasons for our fear. Through observation we'll see that our fears are simply a series of recurring thoughts, feelings, and emotions, and a mirror of how we believe life should or shouldn't be. It can also be how we believe others should or shouldn't be, or how it used to be in our past, or how we expect the future to be, or how we can manipulate people and our circumstances to get what we want. None of these have anything at all to do with what's really happening right now at this moment, and that's the only thing that truly matters. That's the only thing that's truly real.

The only things truly holding our fears in place are our own beliefs. Self-observation is the key to releasing those fears. Fear exists only in our thoughts, feelings, emotions and actions. Amazing, isn't it, to be afraid of our own thoughts and feelings!

Self-observation means "the gathering of information about ourselves for analysis." Without gathering data we don't even know what needs transforming. Self-observation is about making our fears and other nonresourceful feelings and emotions conscious, instead of going round and round on our mental merry-go-round trying to look and feel better while at the same time avoiding the real issues. Avoiding these feelings causes them to become escapist behaviors, which creates further suppression, which in turn strengthens the fear, allowing it to surface later.

We attempt to avoid our feelings so we can escape the pain of who we believe we've become. Feeling guilty or depressed about who we believe we've become is even an escape. Only when we begin to experience ourselves as we truly are do these nonsupportive feelings and behaviors begin to dissolve. When we truly back away, investigate and become more self-observant, and when we begin to peel off those painful emotional layers, only then do we truly begin to discover who we really are. When we begin to observe ourselves, we begin to see clearly what is, and we'll also realize that what was can't be changed. We can always learn more by looking inward for a moment than we can by looking outward for a lifetime.

Whereas the woman in the beginning of the chapter wanted a system to transform her life, all she really needed to do was to look within and to see reality clearly. She would see first that she was in control of her own life; second, what she was hanging on to that needed resolution; and third, that she had the power to change and transform her own life.

Some believe that self-observation is a difficult thing. In reality, nothing is simpler. If we can walk across the room and observe ourself doing so, at that moment we are in a state of observation, and at that moment we are free. But if we cannot bring up our depression, observe it and let it go, then we are not free and can never be free. But if we can observe our depression and allow ourselves to experience it, we have let it go. On the other hand, if we observe our depression, then attempt to disassociate ourselves from it through some sort of positive thinking or some other mental maneuver, we are only burying it deeper, leaving it to rear its head again at a later time.

If we truly want transformation, we must start today to observe our every thought, feeling, emotion, word and action. If we discover ourselves speaking and acting in a certain way, then we must realize that we have some underlying feeling and belief causing us to speak and act that way. Real transformation only takes place when we let go of the feeling that holds the belief in place.

I remember a woman in one of my classes who believed that letting go wouldn't help her solve her problem. She had two things to deal with. One was that I had to get her to change her belief that letting go wouldn't help her. All the talking in the world wouldn't have changed her mind. I went to work on her real issue, which was her feeling of doubt that letting go even worked at all. Once I helped her to let go of her doubt about letting go, she was now convinced, from experience, that letting go did work after all. We could then move to the real issue, which was her fear of letting go. She was afraid because she didn't know what was going to take the place of her fear. She discovered that she was using her fear as a form of protection, or really as an excuse for staying stuck in her old ways where she felt comfortable.

Observation Creates Reality

In order to make permanent change, we must begin to observe

- how we are when we're alone
- how we are in an uncomfortable situation
- how we are in our relationships
- how we make love
- how we are around people
- how we are at work

We should observe everything about ourselves.

We don't have to stop everything we're doing just in order to observe ourselves. However, when you're involved in an activity, you cannot stop and observe. If you happen to be doing nothing, you can simply observe yourself doing nothing; you may be surprised at your discoveries. Any aspect of ourselves that we don't observe remains unclear. Without self-observation everything will always seem to be outside our control. Self-observation lets us figure out our nonproductive programming and make conscious that which has been unconscious. Self-observation only means developing the habit of checking in with ourselves before taking action.

There is no reality in the absence of observation. Observation creates reality.

I remember a few months ago when I was on the way to the airport and running late. The traffic was at a standstill. It seemed to me that all that traffic was there to hold me up, to interfere with my sanity. I became totally caught up in the traffic and truly felt that it was all there just to slow me down. I felt as if I were trapped on the freeway with nowhere to turn. What I really needed to do was to observe my problem from a higher perspective. What I found through self-observation was that impatience was my real issue, not the traffic. It was almost like a miracle. As soon as I let go of my impatient feeling and accepted that I was stuck in traffic and there was nothing I could do about it, the traffic seemed to begin to move right along. Not only that, but I made it to the airport in plenty of time.

Imagine you are standing in the middle of the freeway between two lanes of traffic. There is traffic about a foot on either side of you traveling at eighty miles per hour. You probably wouldn't feel very comfortable, would you? In fact, you would more than likely feel immobilized and afraid to move at all. You are aware of your surroundings and you don't like them. That's called self-awareness.

What if you step on to the curb and observe the traffic? It wouldn't feel quite so intimidating, would it? You would still be aware of the traffic, but from a higher viewpoint, where you could see the real truth. What if you backed off a little further and observed the traffic from 500 feet in the air? It would even appear a lot less threatening, wouldn't it? What if you observed the traffic from an airplane? It would look like a beautiful rainbow-colored ribbon woven through the landscape. From that level of observation, it wouldn't seem like a threat at all, would it? That's called observation. Self-awareness is knowing you're in it, whereas self-observation is separating yourself from it so you can see the real issue and accept it for what it is or take resourceful action to make a change.

When we observe with a panoramic view, we start to see that the traffic is just traffic, and not out to get us. By observing our own life from a higher perspective, we begin to see places where we're challenged as just a part of our life—not good or bad, but just part of life. After a while, by being more self-observant and letting go, we eventually reach a place where we accept all that we see as the gift that it is. We can then begin to enjoy life and not feel trapped, instead of spending all our time trying to make life something that it's not. We begin to see that our fears are gifts telling us that there is something we need to observe and let go. The more we observe our own actions and nonresourceful feelings, the more our problems lose their hold and begin to wither away from lack of attention. The more the energy from the feeling is released, the less attention and energy will be spent on the issue. The less attention we give it, the more it weakens its hold on us.

Where Attention Goes, Energy Flows

Whatever we focus our attention on is what we create. Where the attention goes the energy flows, and where energy flows manifestation takes place.

It takes three things to change: intention, willingness and commitment. Intention is the starting place. You have to want to change. Willingness is the next step. I remember a couple attending one of my classes a few years ago. They were apparently involved in some sort of conflict. She was clearly holding some resentment toward her husband. During one of the exercises I asked her if she liked feeling that way, and she answered, "No, I don't." Then I asked if she would like to let that feeling go. She answered yes very hesitantly. Then I asked if she was willing to let it go. She answered very quickly, "No! No, I'm not willing to let it go at all, not now, not ever!" And I said, "Fine, let's move on to the next person."

You see, without willingness, there's no need to proceed any further. A few months later I heard that the couple had filed for a divorce. When one holds on to that kind of resentment, there's no room left for resourceful solutions to come forth. There's no room for healing to take place.

It takes a lot of courage to observe what is really happening, to observe it from a higher place and then be willing to let it go. However, it takes a lot more courage to take responsibility than to say, "No. I'm not willing to take a closer look."

It doesn't take any time at all to learn to observe and to let go, as one might think. But it may take some time, and certainly a lot of courage, to make the permanent desired change. Anyone can learn it. We all learned to walk, to talk, to put on our clothes, to tie our shoes, to drive a car, etc. I remember observing my dad driving the car when I was about fourteen. It seemed so easy. When I started learning to drive, it seemed so scary. The steering wheel seemed so big. I couldn't seem to get the brake, clutch and gas pedals to work just right. Remember the first time you attempted to drive a car? You knew what the gas, brake and gearshift were for, but they didn't seem to work as easily as you thought they would. Over time, it grew more and more comfortable until one day, without even noticing, driving a car became almost automatic. After a period of time, you hardly even had to think about it. The same goes for self-observation and letting go. After you do it for a while, it becomes second nature. Which do you think would be more productive, walking 200 miles or driving your car? Which do you think would be more productive, letting go or continuing to hang on and do it the old way?

We've all done many things that seemed impossible in the beginning. I remember when my brother was teaching me to swim. Every time I would try to swim, I sank like a rock. I couldn't figure out how it all worked. I couldn't make my hands and feet move together, keep my head above water and breathe at the same time. I thought I would never get it!

I must have swallowed 200 gallons of water in the process, but finally with a lot of practice I learned to swim. Why did I do it? It's simple. I had the intention, willingness and courage to commit myself to the process of learning. Sure it was scary, but I wanted to swim more than I was willing to stand on the side and watch others having all the fun.

Let's say you wanted to be a skier. You could just call yourself a skier and never go to the slopes. Or you could borrow some skis and give it a try. However, if you were truly serious about being a skier, you could buy your own skis, take a few lessons, and ski when you had the time. Now, if you wanted to become even better, you could take a few more lessons and go skiing regularly. On the other hand, if you wanted to become a master skier, what would you do? You would hire the best instructor you could find, commit your life to learning, practice every moment you could and ski at every opportunity.

We should realize that our life is as it is because of the choices we have made. We may say, "I don't have time to observe, to become aware or to let go," and that's all right, but it's really good to know that we're the ones in charge. It's good to know that we are the ones making the decisions about what we will and won't do. It's important to observe, to let go only when we want to, not out of feeling obligated or from a sense of guilt for not doing it. We should make a choice to become more self-observant and to let go because we want to, not out of a sense of obligation.

I know one thing for sure. When we become observers of our own beliefs and actions, only then can we break free of the old habits that limit our range of possibilities. And when we begin to see even a glimpse of that which we really are outside those old patterns, they will begin to wither away. On the other hand, if we believe that life is difficult and we choose not to observe our own actions, then our own point of reference regarding life will be "Life is difficult." Not only that, but our point of reference will remain so until we realize through our own observation, that this belief that "life is difficult" has not always been a part of our belief system. We must realize that this belief has become our filtering system for all our incoming data about how life is, and all our outgoing data and perceptions that we project out to others as well. Most importantly, we need to know that only we have the power to change that belief and put an end to our filtering system, our belief that life is hard.

Take a moment and try this exercise. Close your eyes and relax. Now recall an incident in your past that upset you. Maybe you missed your plane, you were really late for an important appointment or you had an argument with someone. Visualize yourself in the middle of the incident. Recreate it with all the same feelings and emotions. Next, as you are reexperiencing the incident, begin to observe yourself in the situation. In other words, there's the "you" in the situation, and there's the "you" that's *observing* it. As you observe all your thoughts, feelings and emotions, begin to notice if there's any difference in each situation—being *in* the experience versus being the *observer* of the experience. Try this the next time you get upset about something or at someone. Once you stop and observe your feelings, you'll notice an immediate improvement in how you feel and in your circumstances as well.

I recently entered into a business agreement with a friend. About a year later we realized that there was a point that needed to be better clarified within our agreement regarding his compensation. He asked if I would be willing to make that revision. I agreed to do so.

As the agreement was passed back and forth several times to make sure everything was correct, he began to want to change other things within the agreement. Before long it became something totally different from the agreement when it started. He began to argue about everything, wanting more than we had originally agreed upon in several areas. Each time a revision was made to satisfy him, he became even more demanding and even angry. As his correspondence grew angrier, I found myself getting angry as well.

The next thing I knew, he had hired an attorney to represent him, claiming that if I didn't agree with everything he wanted, he was going to take legal action to gain total control of the project. What started as a friendly business arrangement was now looking like it could turn into a legal battle.

I suddenly found myself feeling taken advantage of on the whole deal. I began to get angry about the whole situation and the more I thought about it, the angrier I became.

I explained the problem to my wife. She asked me how I felt about it. I said that I felt hurt, betrayed and angry.

Right away I saw what I was doing. I was buying into his control drama, instead of being resourceful and finding a solution to the problem. As soon as I realized that it was his problem, his need to be in control so that he would have more acceptance, I could let go of my hurt feeling, and at the same time my anger went away. As soon as I released my need to control him, which was causing my anger, I discovered a solution to the problem.

Once we identify with a feeling such as anger, for example, we lose our ability to see a resourceful solution to the situation. We remain stuck in the problem. More and more as we begin to catch ourselves in nonresourceful situations and observe our own actions, we'll know that we are in transition between behavior patterns.

A person who is habitually angry probably doesn't see himself as an angry person; in fact, he probably doesn't see himself at all. But if he catches himself even once, he has made the first step in changing the belief or habit pattern that causes his anger. When we make a mistake and catch ourselves in it, the end result is real growth.

A word of caution. Beating ourselves up for making a mistake is not the answer. In other words, we shouldn't use self-observation for self-punishment. Don't blame yourself or anyone else for how you feel. It isn't anyone's fault, it's just what's happening. Nonresourceful feelings, emotions and events in our lives show up in order to facilitate our own growth. We develop the capacity to improve ourselves by developing a greater understanding of who we are. Our painful feelings open up possibilities for a new future by giving us new choices.

Conformity or Nonconformity

Most people believe themselves to be victims of some sort of cruel fate. They think their misery is caused by their unhappiness, when in reality their unhappiness is caused by their complaints about their misery. On the other hand, their complaints are caused by some underlying belief about what they think happiness should be. And because of their fear of finding out that they may have been wrong all these years, they just avoid the issue altogether.

We put off facing our fears, as well as our difficult tasks, because we are always bouncing back and forth between conformity and nonconformity. Let's say that we arrive at work in the morning and we know that we have a difficult issue we need to confront—one we really don't want to. Come afternoon we suddenly realize that we still haven't done it. We've found fifty things to do, none of which included confronting the issue. Our initial response upon arriving at work was that we should do it right away. We're the boss and it's our job and we have to do it. That's called conformity. Our next response is that I'm the boss and I don't have to do it, or I can do it later. That's called nonconformity. The instant we step back, observe both sides and begin to see what we're doing, we confront the issue. However, if we never take the time to observe, we may put off taking any action at all. We don't even realize that we're putting it off in the first place. Self-observation lets us understand the maze we are caught up in.

By being self-observant, the first thing we see is what we are doing. The second thing we see is a resourceful solution. We'll begin to see how we swing between conformity and nonconformity, caught between a resourceful and non-resourceful state. By becoming more self-observant we'll realize that we are the one pushing our own swing.

So what's the solution? The solution is to resolve the problem by experiencing what we don't want to experience. We should feel the fear and surrender to the experience. When we surrender to the experience, everything will begin to shift, allowing us to see clearly what needs to be done.

We always want to cling to the familiar, which seems to be less painful. If we want to become a serious observer, we'll need to open ourselves to the experience and begin to become more aware of when we get on the swing, and even more importantly that we're the one pushing it.

Try this self-observation exercise to help you gain a new perspective. Recall a nonresourceful situation in your life.

Now imagine what you looked like in that situation. Next imagine that a mirror is right in front of you. Observe your movements, posture, gestures and the expression on your face. Now, ask yourself why you have created this obstacle in your life. See it as if you are seeing it for the very first time. Now, write down what you see. Next write down how you feel. How you feel is much more important than what you think or see. How do you feel right now? What message are you receiving regarding how you feel? What do you need to let go of? What action do you need to take? If we don't stop to see the truth, we avoid—or suppress—how we feel altogether.

One of the most common emotions people experience when they begin to confront their own issues is fear. When we say, "I'm afraid," we become consumed by our fear: an endless cycle of thought, beliefs and feelings all feeding one another. Our fear feeds the belief, and the belief feeds the fear, which ends up causing an endless loop of fearful reactions to the situation.

I'm afraid I'm going to lose my job. This may trigger *I'm afraid I won't have enough money to live.* This may trigger *I'm afraid I won't be able to get another job. I'm afraid that losing my job will affect my relationship. I'm afraid if that happens, he/she will leave me, and I'll be all alone.* The real fear is not of losing your job, but rather of loneliness.

Here's the solution. When you observe the first fearful feeling as it arises, such as "I'm afraid I'll lose my job," ask yourself this question: "From where does this thought or feeling originate?"

Once you as the aware observer begin to understand that you are not your thoughts, beliefs and feelings, but rather the observer of these things, a greater sense of clarity will come forth.

Some ask, "How do I know if I'm observing or not?" If we were identical to our feelings or thoughts, we couldn't observe them or even know they existed. Observation and knowing about something suggest a separation between it and us. We can observe ourselves flying in an airplane, but that certainly doesn't make us an airplane. There is no reality in the absence of observation. Observation creates reality. In other words, we create our own reality through what we observe . . . or don't observe. If we continue to observe from the false reality of our own outdated beliefs, that is what we will continue to create.

Awareness Versus Observation

There's a difference between awareness and observation. Basically we use our awareness to observe. Self-observation is the capacity to go beyond our mind, where we can observe both our thoughts and emotions. Awareness and observation are both intellectual functions of the mind.

The mind does not connect to our feelings; however, one does influence the other. If we feel anxious, for example, we can consciously choose to use our awareness to think good thoughts or to observe what we are feeling, which is a function of the intellect. We can think good, clear thoughts all we want, but if we don't stop, observe how we feel and let go of our anxiety, before very long we will be entertaining unclear, fearful thoughts once again.

Our conscious mind is the part of us that is consciously aware of internal and external input from our memories, intuition, thinking, the flow of ideas, etc. It is also aware of all our senses: sight, sound, touch, smell, taste and movement. The conscious mind sits on the fence between the inner and outer world. Its primary function is making decisions through the use of intuition, feelings, and attention and interpreting what it sees. The main decision the conscious mind has to make—out of literally thousands of things it has to be aware of—is where to focus its attention.

If we want 100 percent self-awareness, the conscious mind must be in a state of total inaction—in other words, doing nothing, as in a meditative state. We cannot watch television, drive a car or read a book, and at the same time be 100 percent aware.

Taking action, on the other hand, requires excluding other things. If we want to do a specific thing, we have to exclude other things. We must make a decision. Do we intend to push on the brake or push on the gas? One or the other has to be excluded. We cannot act on everything at once. To increase our awareness of one thing requires decreasing our awareness of another. One of the functions of our conscious mind is to make decisions in order to improve our skills, knowledge and effectiveness. We must decide what's important and what's not important, based on our intentions. We must choose what feelings, beliefs, behaviors, etc., no longer serve us, and we must decide from that act of observation which ones we need to let go. Our conscious mind keeps our intention on target, directs our awareness and our activities. When we want to do a certain thing, the mind begins with our intention, followed by our awareness, which focuses our attention on the opportunities and circumstances around us. The mind directs our actions where they need to go in order to achieve our desired intention.

As an example, let's say I decided I wanted to purchase a new car. I can see and feel myself driving it. My intent is strong. Next I noticed my awareness kicking in. I start to become aware of all the BMW 740s on the road similar to the one I want. Finally I have to decide that white is the color I want. Next comes action. I have to go to a dealer to purchase the car. Which dealer do I go to? A BMW dealer, of course. What color will I settle for? Nothing less than white! Why? That is my intention. If I have a weak intention, I might end up at a Chevrolet dealership buying a green Monte Carlo.

Self-observation is a function of the conscious mind. Does this thought, feeling, emotion or behavior support my intention, or is it moving me further away? Is it resourceful or nonresourceful? That's a conscious choice. We can think positively all we want, but if our intention is weak, nothing happens, except maybe going around in circles.

Feelings are the magnets that attract, and intention is held in place by feelings. Our thinking process is only the mechanism that chooses the direction we want to take.

Using positive thinking as a means to stay focused only further suppresses the nonsupportive feeling that keeps our old beliefs alive. We can't replace a negative emotion with a positive thought. Eventually the emotion will win out.

The key to staying on purpose is self-observation: observing our every thought, language, feeling and behavior, observing the TV show going on in our head. You know the one I'm talking about. Everyone has one. It's going on right now. Stop for a moment and observe your own drama. Some are *Searching for Tomorrow.* For some it's *General Hospital.* For others it's *The Young and the Restless* or maybe *The Guiding Light.* Some are attached to watching old reruns, playing the same story over and over again. Some are into silent movies. Others watch the news looking for something exciting to broadcast to others. You know the shows I'm talking about. Just sit back on occasion and observe your own drama. Look at all the players you've assembled to assist you in playing out your drama. Who are the main star, co-star and victim? Who's the villain? The whole cast of characters, even the extras walking across the street, are part of your drama. The part that others play in your drama can only be understood to the degree that you understand yourself.

Here's the really good news: we are the scriptwriters! We can write a new story line, cast the characters, get rid of the victim, change the players and redesign the scenery. We can write a love story or a story of success and happiness, create a whole new set or a new location shoot, hire new extras. We can create anything our heart desires, anything we can imagine. After all, we imagined the drama we're now living. How do you think it was created in the first place? The question is what does your heart desire? What do you want to create?

Rewrite Your Drama

Take a moment right now to consider your drama. Label it. Is it one of love, happiness and joy, or is it one of fear, anger, loneliness or depression? Or maybe it's anxiety. That's a good one! Anxiety is when we mix fear, depression and anger. The fear tenses your body and holds you back. The depression tenses your body and pulls you inward. The anger tenses your body and pushes you forward. So we end up going in three directions all at the same time. We are angry for not getting what we want fast enough. We become depressed that we don't have it now, but someone else does. We are afraid to take a step forward because we might lose again. Our fear of not ever having it has immobilized us. We feel like we are going really fast, but nothing seems to be happening except that we are getting very tired! The only way to truly let go of our anxiety is not to speed up, but rather to slow down—or better yet to stop! We need to stop, regroup, get focused, let go of the need to control every outcome, and then move forward, taking action from a state of resourcefulness.

Here's the underlying issue. Our drama is not the problem; it's our pride, our egos. When we're angry, we don't really want to observe it and watch it go away. No, we want to be right! Our ego wants to be right, not to resolve the issue. Why? The ego exists only as a result of our problems. However, it "feeds" on our fears, anger, depression and anxiety. As we focus on those things, the ego gets stronger.

When we step back, observe and let go, we begin to enter a new dimension in which we know exactly what to do, what action to take on the spot in any situation. Not only what actions to take for ourselves, but for the benefit of others.

Try this simple exercise. Pick a day. All day long, observe your thoughts, feelings and behaviors. Observe your own drama. Begin to notice your beliefs about certain issues. You'll be absolutely amazed! Notice the players. Notice the role you play. Then pick another day and observe the drama of the people around you. Notice what role you are playing in other people's dramas. Watch other people's drama at work, at home, on the freeway. Where do you fit in? Are you the controller or the one being controlled? Do you seek to gain acceptance from others? Are you the victim? Do you like the role you have created for yourself? If not, what could you do to change your role?

Someone once asked me which was more important, self-observation or letting go? The answer is that we can't have one without the other. In order to let go, we first must be in a state of self-observation. When we are in a state of self-observation, we are automatically letting go. They work hand in hand. When we become self-observant, that act alone is letting go. As soon as we observe a nonresourceful feeling, we separate ourselves from it, and in turn we peel off a layer of that feeling, decreasing its power over us. For example, it's impossible to observe ourselves in a state of anger and remain angry. Try it. The act of observation in itself releases the anger.

The way to increase your effectiveness at letting go is to increase your effectiveness at self-observation. When we get upset, we have lost our effectiveness at self-observation. You've heard the saying "You can't see the forest for the trees." In other words, we get so caught up in our problems that we aren't open to or can't see the solutions at hand.

You can't remain upset about a situation if you are in a state of self-observation. Why? Because you, the observer—the real you behind the ego—never gets upset. As an observer, you can watch your own drama with interest and curiosity but without getting the least bit upset.

Becoming a consistent and persistent observer is the only answer to remaining resourceful. If we observe, we will one day see life as it truly is. We've all had those moments. We look at a sunset and for those few minutes we have no barriers, no drama. There is just you and the sunset, and for that moment you experience the real you. That's the way life is supposed to be.

Self-defeat in any endeavor doesn't mean that victory doesn't exist; it simply means we approached it incorrectly. On the other hand, through self-observation we become open to other options. As we begin to observe, all our fears and ego-created dramas can be put into proper perspective. Through persistent self-observation, the clouds covering the beautiful landscape and sunset eventually disappear, the pain subsides and fears recede.

You may be asking yourself a question or two at this point. *If I'm always trying to live in the moment, how do I plan for tomorrow? Do I still set goals for my future? How can I live for today and still plan for tomorrow?* We always want to try to figure everything out, don't we? We want to know all the minor details about how tomorrow will be. We want to predict the outcome of that all-important meeting next week. The truth is there is no way in the world to know how tomorrow is going to turn out.

I'm not saying that we should refrain from setting goals or making plans for the future. We certainly want to plan for tomorrow, and we want to plan for that important meeting. But here's the solution to staying resourceful. Don't try to live tomorrow today! Don't attempt to figure out or control an outcome over which you have no control. If you do, you'll miss today, you'll miss what's really going on in your life. Any time you are not living this moment, you are out of this moment, and this moment is where your life is taking place. It's where the real action is!

We always seem to want to drift off into what's going to happen next week or even next year. We start to think about our money problems, our fears and worries about tomorrow. This moves us into a nonresourceful state where there's nothing—I mean *nothing*—going on. There's nothing wrong with planning for the future, but we should avoid getting lost in it. When we are lost in our thoughts about the future or the past, we *are* lost, and we *have* lost! Before we know it, we are at the end of the day, or even worse, the end of our life, and we discover we have only lived a fraction of it. But this is what most of us do. We don't do it just part of the time; we do it a lot of the time. We are constantly trying to eliminate our current problems or current feelings by pushing them away or avoiding them. This approach only wastes our precious time by keeping us stuck in a state of nonresourcefulness where there's nothing going on except our confusion about what to do next.

Label Your Feelings

Begin now and try the following for thirty days. When unwanted feelings arise, step back and observe. Don't just label your feeling "fear," but be more specific: "I'm feeling fearful about losing my job." If you find things happening too fast to deal with them, try stopping for a moment and labeling your feelings: "I'm feeling anxious." Stop for a moment, take a deep breath and let it go. If the same feeling keeps popping up again and again, progress is taking place. If we resist instead of observing an unwanted feeling, three things happen. One, we suppress the feeling, thus allowing it to grow in strength to surface again later. Two, we will miss the gift it offers. Three, we completely miss the moment.

Self-observation and letting go are not passive activities, as many people believe; they are the means to living a life of resourceful action. Letting go is high action and low attachment. When we let go prior to taking action, our action will be reality-based, not action that is created and motivated by our conditioning or by nonsupporting beliefs. Resourceful actions always produce resourceful results.

It's also important to know that through self-observation and letting go we are freeing ourselves from all programming rather than attempting to reprogram. Reprogramming without first letting go of the old programs is like jumping out of the frying pan into the fire. We may think that we have discovered a better program, a better system, but the whole point is not to be run by a program or a system in the first place. All our programs and beliefs create systems that are limiting. By following a system or program, we only become limited by that system or program.

Over time, the conscious choices we once made have become unconscious and automatic programming.

Let's say that as a young man I went to work as a salesperson in telemarketing. It was the worst experience in my working career. I made hundreds of calls, received enormous rejection from prospects and still made no sales. Later I was offered a very good job as a national sales director for a large company. The job paid very well, but I was afraid I couldn't handle it. Even though I had plenty of education and experience and I was perfect in the eyes of the interviewer, the word *sales* frightened me to no end. I was still carrying around my past experience with selling. I was allowing it to affect me today even though it had absolutely nothing to do with the present situation.

We will always suffer unconsciously what we do not face consciously. We can learn more and make more progress in our own development through a day of self-observation than from a lifetime of external circumstances or motivation. Looking outside is only dreaming, while looking inside is waking up.

We have all developed our own automatic patterns, and some are very helpful—like driving a car, putting on our clothes, walking, etc. But what we want to do is to interrupt the nonsupportive patterns. How? By observing them.

I would challenge you to discover just one nonresourceful pattern each week, and to observe it and see what happens. What do you have to lose? You never know—it just may work!

Honesty Is the Only Policy

Another important component of observation is to be honest with ourselves, to admit our true attitudes to ourselves.

I realize that it's hard to have that kind of honesty with ourselves, but we don't have to share it with anyone. No one has to know but us. If we want to truly experience growth, we'll eventually have to admit to ourselves that we are chasing perfection rather than letting go of our imperfections.

Don't try to go too fast. Speed is not the answer. We may increase our speed but at the same time lessen our results. By being patient observers, we'll begin to discover that most of our deadlines, if we truly admit it to ourselves, are deadlines that have been imposed upon us by others, not deadlines we've set for ourselves.

It's also important to take some time for yourself, time when you have nothing at all to do. Observe yourself not being busy. Observe yourself being busy, and let go of the need to be busy all the time. When you do, you'll be surprised at how your creativity, productivity and peace of mind increase.

If you find yourself feeling overwhelmed, the old you may say, "My loneliness overwhelms me." Instead, say to yourself, "Sometimes I decide to be overwhelmed." It's your choice. The nonobserver says, "What do I do now?" The observer says, "What do I need to understand about myself?" One approach is problem-oriented, and the other is solution-oriented. One is resourceful, and the other is nonresourceful.

Observation works in many ways. If we begin to observe any given thing on the face of the planet—a blade of grass, a tree, anything—it can reveal a solution for us.

I once saw a small piece of bread that seemed to be moving on its own across the floor. At closer look, I discovered about six ants all working together to carry the bread back to their anthill. I saw discipline, teamwork, intention, action and consistency. The message from that act of observation was something I really needed: "You can't do everything for yourself, you need a team." As a result of that experience in self-observation, I now have a talented, productive team working with me.

Again, any given thing on the face of the earth can reveal to us the solution to our problems, if we will but observe it and listen to our own inner voice. Try opening a magazine to any page, and see if you can find the solution to a problem you may be experiencing. Look at a person's hand, turn over a card or watch a bird in flight. Whatever you observe, you can find a connection to your own experience, if you are truly open to receiving it.

Begin today to observe, to let go of the old in order to make a place for the new. Begin today to take responsibility—not for how or why your programs and patterns were developed, or what you are experiencing as a result. All of that doesn't matter; it only creates guilt and nonresourcefulness. Instead, observe and ask yourself if the feeling you are experiencing is supportive or nonsupportive. If not, let it go and move on!

We're talking about taking responsibility for observing your own thoughts, feelings, belief systems, language and behaviors. Begin to take responsibility for observing how you feel, letting go of those things that do not empower you and taking resourceful action.

Instead of saying, "Why does this always happen to me?" take the resourceful approach and say, "What feeling am I hanging on to that attracts this painful situation?" Instead of saying, "How do I relieve my anxiety?" say, "What feeling am I hanging on to that's causing me to feel anxious?" Instead of saying, "Why is this person acting this way?" say, "Why should I suffer over how anyone is acting?" Instead of asking, "If God really exists, why doesn't he help me?" try a resourceful solution. Observe yourself feeling sorry for yourself and ask, "How come I have created such a stupid drama for myself, and what do I need to do to make a change?"

Self-knowledge is the only starting point for transformation. The intention to know yourself is the starting point to being happy. You must have the intent to know why you do what you do in order to gain true understanding. Self-understanding requires self-observation, and self-observation must be followed by the discipline to let go and allow the real you to unfold.

Remember, what you see and experience is who you are . . . and who you are is what you'll see and experience. End of story!

5

Avoiding Suppression

Perhaps
if we stopped
beating ourselves up
by hanging on
to our old beliefs,
there would be
no reason to continue
the behavior that leads
to the beating

Most of our needs, as well as all our attachments, result from beliefs. Our beliefs are the filtering system through which we perceive reality. For example, if you believe that pushing against is the way to get rid of fears and achieve happiness and success, and letting go has no bearing on your happiness and success, then letting go will not work for you. The beliefs you hold actually create your reality. We acquire our beliefs in many ways. We develop them as a result of our habit patterns, what we do on a day-to-day basis, and of course through social conditioning. Many beliefs are destructive, irrational, counterproductive and limiting. In fact, all our beliefs are limiting to one degree or another. Our beliefs set the boundaries in life, and therefore we become limited by what we believe we can do.

As we become more aware of the limiting or counterproductive nature of a certain belief, we set out to change it to a more productive and less limiting belief. The difficulty, however, in changing a belief is that we believe it can be changed through some sort of mental process. The reality is that our beliefs are maintained by our own suppressed energy patterns and can't be changed through a mental process. The feeling we hold about any given belief is what maintains that belief and keeps it alive. Letting go of a suppressed or trapped feeling is the only way to release the energy that maintains the belief. Releasing the emotion is the only way a belief can be changed.

For example, a new experience or new knowledge that is unrelated to the past will not, in itself, produce any emotion. On the other hand, if we have a memory pattern or some expectation that relates to some past experience or some belief we already have in place, it will produce emotion.

Pushing the old belief out by force is not the answer either, because the feeling keeping it alive has not been released. By letting go we simply and easily outgrow the belief. We have all outgrown certain beliefs, we would not be where we are today and doing what we're doing. For example, I used to believe that reading was very difficult. It would take me days to get through a book. I could only read at about 140 words a minute, whereas the national average was about 240. I just didn't have the belief that I could ever develop the ability to read much faster at all, and certainly not above the national average.

One day I was introduced to speed-reading. Within ten lessons, I was reading at about 28,000 words a minute. Now I have a new belief system. Why? By virtue of letting go of the old while developing a new emotional experience toward reading.

We can outgrow a belief through experience, or we can choose to outgrow it by letting go of trapped, self-limiting energy patterns. However, if a strong, counterproductive emotion is attached to the belief, it becomes almost impossible to outgrow the belief through new experience.

The universe will always and without question create the realities of our beliefs, both automatically and unconsciously, or automatically and consciously. Therefore, our life becomes a matter of choice, or a matter of chance. We can choose to hang on to our old ways, the ones that are causing us pain, or we can choose to let go of the old and be open for a new and better way. Isn't it good to know that we are the ones in control of making the decisions?

Feelings Create a "Magnetic Pull"

When any energy pattern is locked within holding a belief in place, it is beyond space and time. It will continue to produce the experience of the trapped energy again and again until it is released. The pattern lives in the moment. In other words, if anger was developed in childhood and has not yet been released, it might as well have happened this morning. Even though the feeling was created long ago, if it is not released, it still has power over us in the present.

Trapped energy patterns (feelings) set up a magnetic pull, and until they are released they will continue to attract circumstances in our life that will give us another opportunity to let it go, or to relive it once again.

Emotions do not occur by themselves. Memories or a present-moment experience that remind us in some way about a past experience always trigger all emotional reactions. To say it in another way, memories of past experiences and the trapped feelings attached are the only sources of emotions.

Emotions are trapped energy patterns that are set off by memory responses. No one walks around full of sadness. They walk around focused upon memories—or having new experiences that are in some way related to their past memory of pain—that once again stimulate their trapped energy patterns of sadness.

Everything in the universe is made up of energy or atoms. A tree, a telephone, my clothing, the pen I am holding are all energy—trapped energy. Everything is composed of the same energy, waiting to be molded into something usable.

The feelings we hold inside that we call "nobody loves me" or "I'm afraid" or "I am lonely" are all made from the same energy, and they are just as real, just as physical as the tree outside my window. What would happen to the tree if we set it on fire and burned it to the ground? It would disappear, wouldn't it? Well, yes and no! The physical form of the tree would disappear. But the energy of the tree would still exist. It has been released into usable energy once again.

What happens if heat energy is brought into contact with ice? The ice changes form and becomes water. Now we can drink it. If we apply even more heat than the water can stand, its molecular structure begins to change, and it becomes evaporated water. If we apply even more heat, it begins to boil and becomes steam. The ice, water, vapor and steam change to a higher and higher frequency. As it moves from water to vapor and then to steam, we can even breathe it, but we can no longer drink it, or hold it as we could the water. We didn't add anything at all except a heat source, which in itself is also energy at a higher frequency. When heat is added, the water begins to resonate with the heat, becoming as much like it as it can.

The objective here is to get you to perceive and think of energy in a different way. Energy flows where attention goes. Since everything is energy, there are many energy patterns all around us and of course inside us. The energy patterns we hold inside not only have an influence on our every action, but also on those around us as well.

If we believe ourselves to be victims of circumstances, at any time we can choose to change our belief by letting go of the feeling and emotion that supports it.

Remember when we used to play make-believe as children? Try it. Close your eyes and make believe how you would like your life to be. What came up? And, more importantly, how does that make you feel?

Make-believe, with enough intention, will become a reality. You will begin to "resonate" at that frequency. If you take two components, intention and vehicle, and measure what percentage each plays in producing the results you want, here's what it would look like.

$$INTENTION = 100\%$$
$$VEHICLE = 0\%$$
$$RESULT = 100\%$$

Intention produces the result. Without clear intention there is no need for a vehicle. Intention only comes in 100 percent packages. If we are not 100 percent committed to doing something, then it will not happen. You might say, what happens if I set out to do something and only accomplish half of what I set out to do. Isn't that only 50 percent intention? What it actually means is that you were 100 percent committed to achieving only half of your objective. Without a clear intention, the truth is that we are only playing make-believe.

Thoughts Choose Our Direction

Once we've let go of that nonresourceful feeling, we can now begin to create a new vision for our life with a clear intention.

Our thoughts choose our direction in life. When a thought aligns with our focus of attention, change occurs, just like in the example of heat and ice. The reason our thoughts don't always produce change is that we have a conflicting belief that is stronger that produces a conflicting thought. Our thoughts, whether resourceful or nonresourceful, are held in place by beliefs that are supported by feelings, which are energy patterns. When we learn to let go and defuse the energy patterns, only then can we begin to change the belief. At the same time, our thoughts can become more effective in creating and staying focused on the direction we desire in our lives.

We all spend a lot of time and energy trying to label our feelings, thoughts and emotions. The good ones we try to hang on to, and the bad ones we try to suppress or push away. We'll have a wonderful sense of relief when we begin treating our feelings as just moving, changing energy, especially when we discover that we have absolute control over them.

Sit comfortably for a moment and just relax. Take a few long, slow, deep breaths, and let all your muscles completely relax. Let go of all the tension. Now, in your imagination, attempt to get as angry as you possibly can, while at the same time trying not to tense a single muscle. What you will find is that as long as you remain relaxed, it is impossible to get angry at the same time. A trapped emotion, no matter what it is—anger, fear, sadness—cannot be present without muscle tension.

As we begin to let go, when we can relax at will, we will be able to free ourselves from unwanted emotions. Not only that, but without these emotions present, we'll be able to find more-resourceful solutions to our problems.

I read a story once about a devotee who went before his master and said, "I'm a very angry person, and I want you to help me." The master said, "Show me your anger." The man replied, "Well, right now I'm not angry, I can't show it to you." The master then replied, "Well, then, the anger is obviously not you, since sometimes the anger is not even there."

Anger, like any other emotion, is just energy. It is simply what you are experiencing, not who you are. Any emotion, whether it is anger, sadness or fear is only your identification with a past experience that you have trapped inside and given a name. Think of a time when maybe you dented your car or broke something you really liked. It really felt like *you* were dented or broken, as you went around all day reliving the experience. The bottom line is that we are not our past experiences, we have only become temporarily identified with them. We are whatever we are experiencing right here, right now—nothing more and nothing less.

Memories can be very beneficial to us, but if recalling a memory also brings forth an unpleasant emotional response that is not released, the recall can be harmful to our well-being.

In order to more fully understand this concept, imagine something emotionally painful that happened to you in the past. You, as that person in that time, do not exist in the present moment. In other words, it's not happening to you now. You and whoever might have been involved in your past situation are not in the room with you now. You are only holding the image and the experience in the present moment. In order to resolve this unpleasant experience once and for all, you must let go of the trapped emotional energy surrounding the event. In order to do so, you must first understand that you—not the event—are the one in total control. Not only that, you must be willing to re-experience the event in order to fully let it go. However, many of our past experiences have been brought on by even earlier painful experiences. By re-experiencing and letting go of one feeling, it will weaken and release the energy connected to both.

For example, a man in a workshop was having a problem with his older son. Upon further questioning the man discovered that his grandfather was abusive to his father, his father was abusive to him and he felt angry toward life itself. He blamed everything and everyone for his lack of happiness and success. When he let go of his anger toward his father, his anger and resentment toward life—and his problems with his older son—also disappeared.

When we release any nonresourceful emotion, we will always discover many other connecting emotions surfacing as well. Releasing one provides an incredible opportunity for additional healing and growth.

When we experience the emotion, we stop hanging on, which allows the energy in the trapped feeling to return to its original form, which is just free-flowing energy. Look at it this way: let's use the example of the block of ice again. We'll call the ice the experience from our past. The ice is the trapped energy that we'll call anger. Let's say you realize that through your experience, you have frozen the water, the usable energy, into ice, or anger. Once you realize this you can stop freezing the water and let it be simply flowing water (energy) once again in its original form.

There Is No Past or Future

The present is all there is. There is no past or future. Neither exists. When we recall an experience from the past, what we're really feeling is a psychological response in the present. How severe the experience feels in the present will depend on the vividness of our recollection and the impact of the past experience. Hanging on to a past experience can produce the same physical and emotional response that occurred when the event first happened. Even though it isn't happening to us now, our reaction can be very much the same. In some cases the present-moment experience, because of the repeated suppression of the energy, can even be stronger.

Once we begin to observe this process more, we realize that recalling the unpleasant experience can also drain our energy and make us tense, depressed or unhappy. Recalling past pleasant experiences tends to make us feel happy.

Stop right now and recall a past experience that made you feel sad, angry or unhappy. Notice how that makes you feel. Now, quickly, think of something joyful from your past. You'll notice two things. First, you'll notice how difficult it was to switch from the unhappy to the happy feeling. But once you do make the switch, you'll notice how the experience of joy will uplift you. As you begin to work more and more with the process of self-observation and letting go, you'll see how quickly a change can occur. At one minute you can be feeling nonresourceful, and in a brief instant you'll feel resourceful. All that was required of you was to observe any unwanted emotion and to let it go.

Suppression and Repression

Let's examine suppression and repression of our feelings. Suppression is something everyone does to one degree or another. If we've ever known someone who can no longer relate to others, they have merely been more into suppression than the average person. If someone we know seems more well-balanced, they have suppressed less than average. The only way to truly experience personal growth, in my opinion, is to let go of suppressed energy patterns that are affecting us in a nonresourceful way—in other words, to let go of the feelings and emotions that keep our outdated, self-limiting beliefs intact.

Let's examine exactly how suppression works. Suppression begins with resistance. What you resist grows in strength. Let's say that someone says something to you that you don't like, something that really hurts you, and instead of stating how you feel, you say nothing at all and suppress the feeling. After a while, you forget what happened, but the trapped energy pattern that was created by the experience is still there just the same. You see the person again later and you recall the experience, but once again you say nothing. The result is further suppression. You have strengthened the feeling by not addressing the issue. The degree to which you hang on to an issue will depend upon the degree of emotional impact that occurred when it was created. Suppression will also strengthen the emotional impact the next time the issue returns.

As you continue to resist the feeling by suppressing it, you begin to build a shield that blocks the exchange or flow of energy. The next time you see that person they may sense a wall or a shield around you, and they don't even know why. You may not do it consciously, but it's there just the same.

To carry it even a step further, a year—even ten years—later you may find yourself in a similar situation. Without even realizing it, because the person or situation may remind you of the other person or situation from your past, you put up the same wall and block the exchange. It has become an automatic response. Through suppression we all build shields, or walls, to one degree or another around our feelings so they will not be allowed into consciousness. What we don't realize is that when we don't let the feeling go, it doesn't go away. It remains trapped within us, waiting for that opportune, or should I say inopportune, moment to resurface.

Over time, the habit of resisting our feelings will result in chronic repression. Repression is slightly different from suppression because it is an unconscious response. Our automatic reaction becomes so familiar to us that we suppress without even knowing it.

As we suppress or repress to avoid our pain, we also avoid taking responsibility for our feelings. Responsibility means "response-ability," or "the ability to respond." If we don't take responsibility for our feelings, we have no ability to respond. If we can't respond to how we feel, our feelings have total control over us. And the feelings are what's keeping the beliefs in place that we are trying so desperately to change. We fail to realize that our desperation only strengthens the feeling and reinforces the belief.

When we resist a feeling by withdrawing our awareness, this completes the suppression, which keeps the past feeling alive in the present. We really don't avoid the feeling, as we may believe; instead we build its strength for a later appearance. We believe that it is possible to simply close the door on our pain and remain at peace, but we find this to be a misconception.

We attempt to forcefully exclude pain from our awareness through all sorts of evasive actions such as workaholism, overeating, watching television, getting away to discover our life's purpose, etc. What we are really doing is rejecting ourselves, because the pain is still trapped inside. It is held in storage in a state of limbo, waiting for the right time to resurface and give us another opportunity to deal with it.

Feeling energy is stored in the subconscious, just like a program on the hard drive of a computer. The subconscious is filled with suppressed and trapped nonresourceful programs lying dormant, because they were not properly dealt with when they occurred. We then become misguided by unconscious urges that can lead to self-destructive behaviors. What happens then is that we become attracted to, and even attached to, the wrong people and circumstances, and we reject the right people and circumstances. We become compulsive and even addicted to certain behaviors, in spite of our best intentions.

We don't really want these painful situations in our lives, but we automatically attract them because of our trapped energy patterns. Our lives become more stressful, and even confusing, because of feelings that haven't been addressed properly. As we create a new vision of something happy and joyful in our lives, these visions pass through our subconscious programming to gain support for manifestation and become mixed with these nonresourceful patterns trapped inside, creating even more stress and confusion. We perceive and attract what we are holding inside. We perceive it because that's who we believe we are, and we attract it because that's what we need to attract in order to let go and move past it. When you look at it in this way, your nonresourceful feelings and emotions are the gift that's been perfectly presented to you in order to further your growth.

Feelings Are Rumors That Can Be Stopped

Once we begin to truly observe our nonresourceful feelings and let them go, we'll begin to realize that the world we have been experiencing has been created by our own projections. As an example, a person may perceive the world as a threatening place, and as a result of that belief and supporting feeling, that person will experience the world as a threatening place. Perception is a belief, and a belief is something that you decide is true; it may not be at all.

I knew a man back in the early seventies who believed there was a conspiracy to take control of our lives and turn us all into communists. He had gathered all sorts of supporting data from numerous sources, all of which had the same beliefs as he. He had books, tapes and underground newspapers that all claimed it would be happening within the next five years. Every year he seemed to push the predicted date ahead another year. He's now in his seventies and still claiming that we are all headed for destruction. Who knows, this may be so, but I don't choose to live my life controlled by fear and speculation of what could happen. Anything could happen. The earth could get hit by a giant meteor and all of us be killed instantly! My question is, why waste what time we have left living in fear? Why not live fully with the time we have left? He's wasted his last twenty-seven years with a false belief. He's wasted the last twenty-seven years of his life not living as fully as he might have. He lived his life focused on the future possibilities instead of the present moment.

We all take our own individual situations very seriously, and we don't even suspect for a moment that we create our own world through what we project. When any nonresourceful feeling or situation arises, we should automatically assume that it is the result of our own projections.

Any sort of tension in our lives is an unresolved experience we are holding inside. Look at tension as an alarm clock that's telling you it's time to let go. When a nonresourceful feeling appears, stop. Observe it with silent strength. The act of self-observation will turn off your alarm clock. Next, take a moment and determine the outcome if you proceed, realizing that the next action you take will be a seed moment. In other words, it will create a new direction and new outcomes in your life.

Feelings are a lot like rumors. Rumors are the rehashing of something that has happened in the past. It seems real because we are discussing it now, and we are probably doing it with a lot of emotion as well, which makes it seem even more real than real itself. Nonresourceful feelings are nothing more than the resurfacing of a past experience in the form of an emotion that needs resolving.

Remember that it's not what happens that's important. It's how we perceive what happens—and the actions we take based upon our perceptions of what's happening—that really matters.

Avoiding Emotional Hooks

Let's look at some of our favorite ways of suppressing and repressing our feelings. Read the following list carefully and see if you can identify with any of them. Keep in mind that just because you may do some of these things doesn't necessarily mean that you are using them as a form of suppression. However, if you find that you are doing any one of them to an extreme, it may be worth examining a little more closely.

Excessive television viewing
Oversocializing
Excessive use of alcohol/drugs
Smoking
Overorganizing
Overintellectualizing
Excessive sleeping
Habitually overeating
Making lists
Workaholism
Excessive cleaning
An inability to be alone and quiet
Always seeking highs
Procrastination
Blame
Criticizing others
Overspending
Motivation

Let's look at a few of the items on the above list in more detail.

Excessive Television Viewing

Begin to notice how much television you watch daily. It's estimated that the average family in the United States watches television more than eight hours a day. Is it any wonder that families have difficulty communicating? I'm not saying that television is all bad. It's not. Many programs are very good.

Television is not an intellectual process, as we may think. It's an emotional process. Virtually all programs are targeted toward our emotions. Even many educational programs, such as wild animal documentaries, are aimed at violence and killing amongst other species. We are attracted to certain programs because of the feelings we hold inside and how we perceive our world.

We see something on a five-second news update. "A glass of red wine consumed daily may reduce the risk of heart attack, tonight on the ten o'clock news!" So we can't wait till 10:00 so that we can gain support for our drinking that extra glass or two of wine every day. All they really want us to do is watch the news. They are looking for any emotional hook they can find that will make us tune in at 10:00. Observe the brief news clips that try to hook you into watching. Notice their emotional slant.

As you watch television, notice how the television shows target the dramas we are all living. They show hurt, pain, family problems, sickness and death. Begin to notice your own dramas as you watch. Begin to notice when you turn on the television and why. Begin to notice which shows you are more drawn to watching.

I'm not saying not to watch TV. I'm suggesting that you become more self-observant about what you watch and why. Are you watching television to support and suppress a feeling or to avoid an issue? Every time you turn on the TV, stop and ask yourself, "Do I really want to watch this program?" If the answer is yes, then watch it without any guilt. If the answer is no, then leave it off and look for the feeling that needs resolving. Find the feeling that caused you to want to turn it on in the first place.

Oversocializing

Socializing can be great, unless we feel that we have to be with other people all the time to be happy. If that is the case, we should ask ourselves, "What feeling am I hanging on to that causes me to need to always be around people?" You may discover that loneliness is the issue, or maybe a need for acceptance. If you find yourself with a need to socialize a lot, observe yourself in a social situation, and begin to notice who you are socializing with and why.

Making Lists

Twenty-five years ago I used to be a list-making junkie. I would go into an office-supply store and hang out for hours, looking for things I could use for making lists and keeping track of my affairs. I bought planners, game plans and calendars. I had a day-at-a-glance, a week-at-a-glance, a month-at-a-glance; I even had a five-year-at-a-glance. If it had been available I probably would have had a thirty-seconds-at-a-glance! I had things that allowed me to make lists of my lists. I had calendars to keep track of my calendars. Lists are all right, unless you are using them to avoid some feeling. What I discovered is that I used my list-making as a means of avoiding my fear of taking action. I knew that if I took action and it didn't work, then I would have to take responsibility for the results I produced. But if I took no action I could just claim that I didn't have the time or that I was getting ready to take action as soon as . . .

Take a look at your list and learn to see what's really important, and what's there simply to avoid a feeling. Look at your to-do list today and ask yourself, "Is this tension-relieving or is it truly goal-achieving?" In other words, is it taking you closer to how you want your life to be, or is it moving you further away? It's either resourceful or non-resourceful.

Workaholism

If we are consistently working twelve to fourteen hours daily, we could be considered a workaholic. Imagine this scenario: you are on your deathbed and your last words are, "I wish I had spent more time at the office." I seriously doubt that that would be the case. Workaholism can create a one-sided life by excluding many other areas: family, relationships, personal, health. How would you like to work really hard, become really rich, and then get sick and die because you didn't take good care of your health? That wouldn't be very much fun, would it? I heard it explained another way: imagine that each area of your life is a ball. There is a ball for health, finances, career, spirituality, family and relationships. If you drop the ball that represents your career or finances, it can always bounce back. On the other hand, dropping any of the other balls can do irreparable damage. In other words, they may never bounce back. So it makes good sense to keep all the areas of your life in balance.

As we become more self-observant, we realize that being a workaholic is nothing more than suppressing a feeling. There's always a feeling that needs to be dealt with in some way. Notice what and how you are suppressing. You'll begin to experience the real value of letting go of nonresourceful feelings. You'll discover what spending time in a resourceful state really means. Resourcefulness is where the action is. Resourcefulness is where everything gets accomplished.

And I mean everything! Whatever we accomplish in our lives, we are doing so as a result of the amount of time we are spending in a resourceful state. If we are currently resourceful 20 percent of the time and we're working sixteen hours a day to get our work accomplished, what would happen if we could increase our resourcefulness to, say, 40 percent? Here's what would happen. We would now accomplish our job in eight hours instead of sixteen. So by letting go of nonresourceful feelings, we could not only eliminate our workaholism, but we could actually get more accomplished at the same time.

Procrastination

We'll put this one off till later. Just kidding!

Procrastination is another way many people suppress their feelings. It's most often brought on by fear, the fear of success or the fear of failure. We may be afraid of doing it wrong. We may be afraid of not being approved of if it doesn't work the way we plan, or maybe afraid of taking responsibility. Procrastination is most often an unconscious suppression. However, when we suppress through procrastination, there is always a part of us that is aware that we are suppressing.

Chronic suppression can lead to repression, where the acts of both feeling and avoiding a feeling become unconscious. Suppression is basically self-rejection, and repression is just a much more serious form of self-rejection. With repression, which is an automatic response, we become totally out of touch with ourselves and our feelings. Eventually, repression can create an addictive cycle, resulting in anxiety, self-destructive behaviors and even physical illnesses. If we lead a fairly normal life, we all participate in a certain amount of repression. This is normal. However, as we begin to practice more self-observation and address the feelings on more of a conscious level, we'll discover previously repressed feelings beginning to surface, giving us a chance to process them more easily.

Our natural instinct is to avoid pain; therefore, we resist painful feelings. Resistance is just another way that we suppress our feelings. We assume that a painful feeling can be avoided by turning away from it. If someone loses a loved one, for example, their sadness and loss is so overwhelming, so painful that they don't feel they can deal with it. They begin to apply all sorts of avoidance tactics in order to not feel the pain. They begin to read all the time or watch an excessive amount of television, and after a while they become addicted to their act of avoidance. Resistance has become one of the most overused causes of suppression and can lead to addiction.

We must become more observant of when we resist and instead begin to condition ourselves to confront and accept our painful feelings as they arise. In order to release a feeling, we must fully experience the feeling as it arises as an emotion. The more we actually experience and release unwanted feelings and emotions, the more we'll find our personal boundaries and the experience of self-love expanding as well. As we become more accepting of our feelings instead of resisting and suppressing them, we'll discover the very nature of our feelings changing as well. By allowing our nonresourceful feelings to come up instead of suppressing them, over time they will become neutralized, allowing our energy to flow freely once again. We'll raise our threshold of emotional pain, and we'll eventually reduce the amount of pain we have in our lives. On the other hand, by avoiding or suppressing our pain, we lower the amount of emotional pain we can handle, and we can then never get away from it. The more we suppress, the more we'll have to deal with, and the greater the chance that the feeling will continue to surface more often and with more intensity.

As an example, let's take a person with a short fuse who gets upset and angry very easily. Chances are, if you looked back into that person's past, you would discover some sort of feeling of being out of control earlier in life. Maybe divorced parents, a death of one parent at an early age, or maybe even abuse, which left them feeling out of control. Every time a situation came up that left them feeling out of control, they might become angry until they regain control of the situation. The situation probably doesn't even have anything to do with, or even any relation whatsoever to, their earlier experience. The real issue that needs to be dealt with is the feeling of being out of control, or their need to be in control of everything in their lives. If we heal the present feeling, we will automatically heal the past situation, without even knowing what happened to cause our feeling of being out of control.

Blame

Blame is a major way that we avoid and suppress our feelings. Blame is our way of avoiding responsibility for what happens to us. In other words, we are always looking outside ourselves for the reason we feel the way we do. When we become involved in blaming any person, circumstance or whatever for how we feel, we become blind to how we really feel and to the reality of the situation. We are blinded to the truth. The end result is repression of the feelings, which will eventually cause a repeat performance of a similar circumstance at a later time, or at least a circumstance that will cause the same emotion to arise again.

As an example, if we continually blame an outside circumstance, our job, education, government, etc., for our poor financial condition, we will remain blinded to the real issue. The first step to curing our condition is to let go of the blame that blinds us to seeing the truth of our situation. "The truth will set you free."

Self-acceptance becomes virtually impossible when we are blaming outside circumstances for how we feel. Most often we think that whatever triggered our feeling is the cause, so we look for someone or something upon which to place the blame. Whatever triggered our feeling and our need to blame has really offered us an incredible opportunity to bring up our feeling, to observe it, and to let go of anything nonsupportive.

In certain cultures, a person who blames another for his or her problems is considered unconscious. To become conscious we must move past blame into truly understanding the real cause of our problems, which certainly has very little, if anything, to do with the other person. Understanding the problem does not eliminate it. It simply lets us see more clearly what work actually needs to be done. The first step is to see the truth, otherwise we will continue to perpetuate the lie we are living. And without first seeing the truth, how can we possibly know what needs to be done to correct the problem?

It is extremely important not to blame ourselves. We should place no blame either outside or inside ourselves. Blame is not the issue. Seeing the truth is the issue. The way to handle blame is by recognizing the feeling and seeing the truth behind the blame. So when we feel the urge to blame—either an outside circumstance or person or ourselves—stop! Drop the blame. Look for the feeling supporting the blame. Observe it, and then let it go. Only then is it safe to move forward. It's like coming to an intersection where there's a red light and a sign that reads "right turn on red after stop."

Would you even consider for a moment turning right on a red light without first stopping and seeing the truth of the situation? No, of course not!

Forgiveness is also a major part of releasing blame. True forgiveness is realizing that the other person is not responsible for how we feel. No one can make us feel anything. Our feelings are simply the trigger point that shows us what we need to let go of. Often we try to force ourselves to forgive another. We believe that if we forgive, we are being more loving toward the other person. But this type of forgiveness is just another attempt to avoid or suppress our painful feelings. The reason is that we continue to believe that the other person is responsible for what we are feeling. We think that through forgiving them the problem will go away. This type of forgiveness is only intellectual and defeats the purpose altogether. With this type of forgiveness, we become more out of touch with our own feelings, which causes further repression. At the same time no real forgiveness takes place.

True forgiveness comes with the understanding that the original blame was misdirected in the first place. We are often told to forgive without the understanding that we should take full responsibility for our own feelings. When we blame another for how we feel, what we are really doing is taking on the very issue that we are blaming them for in the first place. If someone did something wrong that made you angry, and you blame them for making you feel that way, your anger actually supports the issue and keeps it alive. Get over it! Let it go and move on.

Blaming ourselves for how we feel is not the answer either. Taking full responsibility for letting go of our resentful feelings is the key to forgiveness. Remember that self-blame and taking responsibility are not the same thing. Many are taught that we are responsible for our own experience and, as a result, may fall into the trap of blaming ourselves rather than others. Regardless of whether we place the blame on someone else or ourselves, we are still rejecting ourselves and therefore blocking our own development and peace of mind. Self-blame is just another form of avoiding or suppressing our feelings instead of taking responsibility for them and releasing them.

Even the expression of feelings can become another form of suppression. The expression of anger does not release the anger, as most believe. When we express anger toward another just to get it off our chest, it is harmful to the giver and the receiver. Once we become aware that the other person is not responsible for how we feel or what we experience, it becomes obvious that taking out our anger on another is not the correct approach to getting rid of it.

It may feel as though someone is making us angry when what is really happening is the person is showing us a way to better understand ourselves and to take full responsibility for how we feel. Blaming someone else or ourselves for how we feel is a distortion of reality and leads to further avoidance of the real truth and more suppression of the feeling. In addition, when we express anger it sets up the law of cause and effect, causing it to return to us at another time in another way.

Expressing our anger may appear to be the correct thing to do. It appears to be much easier than not reacting to others' anger at all. But think about it. Who really wins in an argument? Who wins with anger? The answer is no one. Nobody wins. Both parties lose. It's just a temporary release that does nothing at all except strengthen the original feeling that triggered the anger in the first place.

One evening my wife and I were out to dinner with some friends. One of the group was talking about how much she and her husband argued. She asked my wife how often we argued, and my wife thought for a moment and said, "We've been married for twelve years and we've never had an argument that I can recall." She said, "We've had disagreements and discussions, but never an argument." She said that the reason we never argued was that she didn't have anyone to argue with, because I refused to argue.

The true motive behind anger or arguing is always suppression. Expressing our anger by arguing may feel like a release when in reality it only strengthens the feeling for a later appearance. It's really important to know that when we hurt another in blameful expression, we also hurt ourselves. The attack is just as harmful to the sender as it is to the receiver. Angry people eventually end up destroying themselves.

Another thing to realize is that mentally blaming someone is the same as verbally blaming him or her. Whether we express it or simply think and feel it doesn't really matter. The damage is done either way. Either way we are expressing the emotion, rejecting ourselves and suppressing the real feeling.

Motivation

You may wonder what motivation has to do with the suppression of feelings. Many times motivation may be based upon a sense of lack. In other words, we may have lacked something in our past, money for example, and want to have more of it in the future. If we define the words *lack* and *want,* we'll discover that *lack* is defined as want, and *want* is defined as lack. So basically they are both based in fear, the fear of lack and the fear of not having. What happens with motivation is that we take a past experience of not having, which is based in fear, and project it into the future, wanting it to not happen again, and then experience it in the present. Both are fear-based, and both are taking us out of the moment, where the real experience or real life is taking place.

Let's say that you are in sales, and for the last three months you have had terrible production. Almost everyone you called on didn't buy your product. Now you are into a new month, your boss has gotten you motivated to win an incentive trip to Hawaii. The only problem is, as you begin to make your calls, all you can think about is your recent experience of no sales, and not being able to go on the trip with the rest of your associates. Here we have fear of the past projected into the future, with the anticipation of it happening again, and then experiencing it in the moment. You have just cancelled out your motivation, which was based in fear in the first place.

The reason motivation is short-term is that it has no basis in reality. Motivation is when stimulation meets with resistance. The stimulation from want meets with the resistance from past lack. When the stimulation is gone, the motivation ends. Then a new resistance begins, and that's the one that triggered our need for motivation in the first place. Thus an addictive cycle is born.

Most of us are not aware of what motivates us in the first place. We think that getting money will restore a sense of balance into our lives. We need to become more self-observant as to what is truly motivating us. Most of us seek motivation to avoid the feeling of pain or fear that we need to let go of. We feel that something is missing. Something *is* missing: our own willingness to become more self-observant of our non-resourceful feelings.

We all think that we have certain needs. We must achieve something to finally make us happy. We rationalize our behavior, but the real truth is that we are trying desperately to avoid our feelings. For example, let's say that we are depressed and very lonely. Out of habit our basic response is to suppress the feeling through some sort of diversion such as being around people, entertainment, or perhaps alcohol and other recreational substances. In this case our lack of happiness is really motivating us. While seeking motivation to avoid our loneliness, we reject ourselves. Letting go and experiencing real growth becomes virtually impossible as long as we reject ourselves in this manner.

Avoidance may give us temporary, short-term, patchwork relief from our loneliness, but that's the only motivation it will provide. If we would simply face our depression and let it go, it would eventually disappear completely. It probably won't go away immediately, because we likely need to observe and release our suppressed feelings about the issue. Eventually it will go away.

This doesn't keep us from finding a loving relationship if we're feeling sad and lonely. By letting go of our loneliness rather than suppressing it, we put ourselves in a resourceful state where a loving relationship is much more likely. We experience more self-love and therefore we become more attractive to whoever we seek to attract. Accepting and releasing our nonresourceful feelings leads us to a more balanced state where we are open to receive.

When we don't allow our nonresourceful feelings to surface, which allows us to release them, we are beset by all sorts of self-destructive behavior patterns. Our energy flow becomes restricted, and happiness is repelled rather than attracted to us.

We must increase our awareness of our nonresourceful feelings. We must not suppress them, but accept and experience them. We resolve them not by opposing them or being motivated by them but by releasing them. Only when we accept our feelings can we truly put an end to their compulsive influence on our lives.

Be Patient with Yourself

Being patient with ourselves is critical while we release nonresourceful feelings. Being impatient with ourselves is an insidious form of self-rejection that we completely fail to notice. Impatience is the rejecting of what is happening now, in the moment—rejecting reality. We can never be in the moment when we are impatient with ourselves. Right now—in the moment—is where all experience takes place. All love, resourcefulness, happiness, creativity and productivity take place in the moment. When we are out of the moment, it is impossible to be resourceful. And when we are out of resourcefulness, we are out of touch with reality, out of touch with the truth and out of touch with prosperity in any endeavor—be it at home, at the office, or in relationships.

Impatience is equivalent to anxiety. Anxiety is the absence of relaxation. Being anxious means that we are not accepting what is happening. Anxiety causes us to reject what is happening, thus we reject reality and reject ourselves. When we reject reality, we reject life and we reject ourselves. When we are always anxious to get somewhere, we lose our ability to live life in the moment. The moment is the genuine sole existence of life.

Through self-observation, we see beyond impatience to suppressed feelings that need to be released. Fear, depression and anger surround anxiety. As I mentioned previously, fear tenses our bodies and holds us back. Anger tenses our bodies and pushes us forward. Depression tenses our bodies and pulls us inward. So you could say that with anxiety we are holding back, pushing forward and pulling inward at the same time. Can you see why it's so hard to accomplish anything when in a state of anxiety?

Think about it. What do we most often want to do when in a state of anxiety? We feel like speeding up, don't we? It seems like going faster is the only thing that makes any sense. We feel behind; therefore, the only way to catch up is to go faster. Right? Wrong. Anxiety creates confusion. Speeding up only adds to our confusion. When in a state of anxiety the only thing that will ease our pain is to stop and to observe our anxiety. As we stop and observe, we'll discover the solutions to what it is we are anxious about in the first place.

We all suffer from various forms of self-rejection and anxiety that keep us from breaking free from self-imposed limitations. Be patient. Work on one thing at a time. Defeating self-rejection and anxiety requires only two things: courage and patience. It requires courage not to avoid and suppress pain. It requires patience to slow down and release the feelings one layer at a time. The courage to face our feelings and not suppress them brings us self-love and acceptance. It opens us up to a whole new world of possibilities where we will no longer be dependent upon any other person or thing for our happiness. Self-love appears when we let go of non-love feelings.

Letting go is a lifelong process, not something we do once and for all. But the value of every release of any non-resourceful feeling stays with us for a lifetime. When we let go, we discover who we really are. Our spiritual self is reawakening.

Respect for ourselves, for others and for life overall will begin to grow as we develop the courage to face our nonresourceful feelings. As self-love begins to grow, our love for others also grows.

Real love, real self-love, cannot be thought into existence. It only comes through the acceptance of what we truly are, which is pure love, and letting go of all the feelings that are not self-loving or loving of others.

6

Breaking the Hypnotic Spell of Fear

*Fear
exists
only
in our thoughts.
Amazing isn't it?
We're afraid
of our
own thoughts*

Three are three primary considerations in this chapter: our use of language and its effect on our feelings and emotions.

First let's discuss the power of words, because the language we use produces feelings and emotions. For example, consider the phrases, "I hope," "I'll try," "I think," "I believe" or "I know I can do a certain thing." Each phrase produces different feelings even though many people assume they have the same meaning. To try, to think, to believe and to know: how do these words feel to you? Feel them as you say each of them: to hope, to try, to think, to believe and to know. Which one of these words do you think carries the most power? Let's say for example, that I want to write a book, so I set out to hope to write a book. *To hope* is defined as "to entertain an outcome." What if I set out to "try" to write a book. What do you suppose happens? Would I ever finish the book? I probably would not. Why? Because the word *try* is defined as "to struggle." I am going to "struggle" to write a book. Not a very inspiring approach, is it?

I think I will write a book. To *think* is defined as to contemplate. *I am going to contemplate writing a book.* Still not a very resourceful approach to getting the job done.

I believe I will write a book. To *believe* is defined as to hold an opinion of. *I have an opinion that I will write a book.* Believing will still probably not get the job done.

I know I am going to write a book. To *know* means to feel certain. *I feel certain that I am going to write a book!* Only when we feel certain do we really get the job done.

Our language creates our feelings and emotions, and at the same time our feelings and emotions, not properly dealt with, support our language. We express ourselves based on how we feel, and how we feel influences how we express ourselves.

When you look at it from these five perspectives, which affirmation imparts power and certainty to you? Which approach is the most resourceful? If our feelings attract, and they most certainly do, which statement would be the most likely to get a book written? Is it to entertain, to struggle, to contemplate, to believe or to be certain?

Only when we know will we truly get the job done. Why? Because knowing is seeing and expressing the truth.

Most of us have been programmed to live in our rational minds instead of our feelings. We are actually taught to suppress how we truly feel, to suppress our intuition, our imagination and our creative abilities. The fact is that the words we use and hear are such a part of our everyday language that we tend to believe them without question, rather than experience how we truly feel about what we are saying.

All Words Are Hypnotic

All words hypnotize. A few thousand years ago humans heard only a few words daily. Only in the last two hundred generations or so has this increased to sometimes tens of thousands of words being processed through the average person's head every day. Remember that in Genesis, the origin of all things, the Source, was "The Word."

For example, the dictionary on my desk has over two-thousand pages with an average of fifty to seventy-five words on each page. That's over 150,000 words, many of which have multiple definitions. Words are not just sounds that we can choose to ignore, especially if you speak them. Words influence the behavior of both the person talking and the one listening.

When the ancients referred to hypnotic spell casting, it wasn't their superstitions at work; they were recognizing the hypnotic power of words and how they were communicated. This is the reason, as I have mentioned earlier, that the organization of letters into a word is called "spelling." Words cast spells! They cast a spell on the receiver as well as the sender.

Words are stored in the brain like an erector set. Take the word *freedom,* for example. Your concept and my concept of freedom include words, images, feelings and thoughts that we have stored in our minds and that are associated with the word or concept of freedom. Your concept of freedom is probably totally different from mine.

When one person thinks of freedom, it may differ greatly from another's thought of freedom. To one, freedom might mean having lots of money. For another, freedom might mean taking a walk on the beach every day. Either way, whenever we contemplate the word *freedom,* we become hypnotized by it to one degree or another. In addition we may be able to influence another's concept of freedom simply by communicating our concept of freedom.

We wonder why so many people suffer from emotional distress such as worry, fear, depression and anxiety. It is because we have so many words to communicate and to assimilate daily, words that hypnotize us into a particular state of emotion. Think about it. If we didn't have all those words and all that input to process, would we have stress?

All words carry a vibrational frequency that is either resourceful or nonresourceful, depending upon their use. Resourceful words carry frequencies that are expansive, that lead us closer to self-love and happiness, closer to how we would like our lives to be. Words that are nonresourceful and restrictive lead us away from those things we would love to have in our lives, or lead us away from the experience of greater self-love.

Words such as "I can't," "I don't care," "what's the use" or "it's too late" all create conditions of nonresourcefulness,

206 • BREAKING THE HYPNOTIC SPELL OF FEAR

restricting the flow and taking us away from the happiness, love and peace of mind that we are seeking. On the other hand, words such as "I can," "I know," "I am confident," "I am receptive" and "I am dynamic" are resourceful and supportive. They are expansive, leading us toward our vision of happiness and the experience of self-love.

Words are not just arbitrary sounds that we should ignore. They either expand our use of resourceful energy or they restrict it. Words are the verbal expressions of how we feel, of the person we imagine ourselves to be, of how we perceive the world. They are the result of how we experience the world.

A passing thought, for example, may not necessarily create a result, but when we think it, feel it and then verbalize it, the universe goes to work to manifest it. In other words, the law of attraction is set into motion. Thoughts, verbalized from a nonresourceful feeling or emotional state, have the power to create nonresourceful conditions in our lives. The stronger the emotion behind the word, the greater its effect.

Three universal laws that can't be broken are in effect at all times: the law of restriction, the law of expansion and the law of attraction. When we are in a feeling state of resourcefulness, we are applying the law of expansion, which moves us closer to what we love. When we are in a state of nonresourcefulness, we are applying the law of restriction, moving us into our fears. And no matter what we are feeling, resourceful or nonresourceful, the law of attraction is always at work.

For example, if we have a serious illness and we fear we won't recover, and we believe that we're going to just have to live with it, we may say things like, "I've got the illness, and there's nothing I can do, so what's the use?" If we speak those words, the universe will go to work to honor our wish. We are operating within the laws of restriction and attraction.

Look at it this way. Every word we speak is like a prayer. When we pray with feelings, emotions and belief, we always get what we pray for. So if we believe that happiness is impossible for us, we definitely don't want to verbalize it— in other words, don't pray for it!

When we are in a state of nonresourcefulness, we might want to consider two things. One is to keep our mouth closed! And two, don't verbalize our problems! The idle chatter will propel nonresourceful energy out into the world, which will accentuate and attract those things that we are verbalizing.

So, how do we transform our fears and the feelings that limit us and separate us from love, joy and our true nature? A good starting point is by creating a new language—a language that expresses how we want our lives to be, a language of caring for ourselves and others. We should begin to observe and choose our words with care since words empower us and others. Choose words that expand our energy and attract what we want into our lives.

Look for ways to say things that leave the recipient empowered and feeling better as a result of having contact with you. As a result you will leave yourself feeling empowered as well. Begin to select words that affirm life, that affirm abundance, that affirm love, integrity, commitment and a heartfelt connection to everyone you meet. Vision becomes reality. The words we choose create a vision of how we perceive life. Our perception creates our reality.

The Internal/External Connection

Next, we assume that there is only a casual connection between the internal and the external. We believe that some outer event actually caused us to feel a certain way. Although it may be difficult to perceive, the inner event and the outer event actually happen at the same time. One does not cause the other.

Let's say that someone says something that makes you angry. What really happened is that you already held a feeling trapped inside you in the form of anger, which was created from a past experience. It's not at all related to the current anger you're experiencing or to the person who you believe is making you angry. Simultaneously, the act brings up your anger emotion, giving you the perfect opportunity to let it go. If you have anger and resentment toward another, about something that you believe they are doing to you, the act that you believe they are doing to you, and your anger and resentment created by some past event are meeting at this place and time. Without the trapped anger, the event probably would not have occurred at all. And if it did occur, you would have perceived it differently. Why? Because we see and experience only what we are projecting.

For example, my wife is structured and organized, while I operate more without structure and am less organized. Our children are of course less structured and organized by their very nature. As a result, my wife is more bothered by our children's disorganization. We perceive it differently. It's because we feel different. We are projecting something different; therefore, we will attract or see each situation differently. Without the feeling of needing to have everything in control, we don't feel out of control.

If we are not holding anger, we are not projecting anger, and the situation would not make us angry. Understanding this concept removes the tendency to blame others for their language or actions or how they make you feel. It makes self-acceptance as well as accepting others much easier.

Thoughts Trigger Feelings

Feelings are not always accompanied by outside events; instead a feeling may be triggered by a thought. We often use certain thoughts repeatedly in order to bring up certain feelings that need processing—for example, a feeling of sadness because of the death of someone close to us. We remember being with that person, and as a result of that thought, we experience a sad feeling. The thought serves to bring up the feeling just as an outer event might do. However, it is not the thought that needs processing, but rather the feeling. Even more than that, the emotion (feeling energy in motion) that is surfacing as a result of that feeling needs processing.

A behavior can also serve to bring up feelings that need to be released. If we are compulsive, for example, about keeping our house clean, or having something a certain way, if we become self-observant, we will begin to see the feeling behind our compulsiveness. Our compulsiveness becomes the gift, by offering us a signal that there is something we need to deal with and an emotion that needs releasing.

We can look at a nonresourceful thought, feeling, emotion, behavior or circumstance in this way. See it as an incredible opportunity to let go and to grow. Our feelings and emotions are not something to be feared, or to suppress in order to avoid the pain. They are truly a gift. In order to truly grow, it is necessary to feel the pain, allow the emotion to surface, observe it and then let it go. Anything we cling to will eventually cause us pain.

It's also important to know the difference between thoughts and feelings. When we are working with feelings, we are working with energy. A thought, on the other hand, doesn't always have a charged feeling or any energy, for that matter, behind it. Nonresourceful feelings are always energy-based, which produce emotions, and letting go of the emotion attached to the feeling serves to loosen the energy blocks.

Think of a time when you made the statement, "Wow, that was a relief!" What happened was that you let go of your fear, your emotion. You let go of a nonresourceful energy block.

A lot of therapies attempt to go back into the past to uncover suppressed feelings and their causes. Going into the past is not really necessary. When we are working with present energy that was created from a past experience which is always the case, letting go of the present feeling will automatically heal the past. Why? Because the past and present are connected. The past experience is what's causing us, either directly or indirectly, to feel what we are feeling today. For this reason, when we let go of a present feeling, we automatically heal a past pain.

Pure feelings are not filtered through past experiences. For example, you may feel happy, alive or loving. These are all pure feelings with no emotional connection to the past. If we are aware of a pure feeling, there is no need to let it go, because with a pure feeling we are already in the experience of the moment. Also with a pure feeling we will not experience stress. Why? Simply because there is no stress in the moment. Stress comes from emotions, and emotions are created in present time, from a trapped feeling, as a result of a past experience.

Suppressed past feelings can be and are projected into present situations. In this way looking at the present can also be looking at the past, whereas looking at the past is not ever living in the present, it is simply reliving the past all over again. Letting go of a past experience in the present serves to heal the past.

Imagine that you are taking a walk out of doors. Everything feels perfect. There is no feeling of stress, just you and nature. You are feeling wonderful! Then suddenly you remember a stressful situation at the office. The next thing you know, you are feeling stressed out, and everything no longer seems so perfect. Remember, there is no stress in the moment. The only time stress exists is when we bring the past into the present, reliving it once again.

Eliminating Worry

Let's examine worry. Worry is a unique fear condition. Worry is thinking about what we are feeling instead of feeling the feeling. Instead of feeling the fear, we are thinking about what we fear. Worry is always based in some way on a past experience and some related belief we hold about that experience.

Let's say that we are worried about our teenager going to the senior prom. We are afraid they are going to stay out all night, possibly drinking and getting into trouble. The reason we are worried is that we may have a belief that says that's what teenagers do at senior proms. And why do you suppose we feel that way? Maybe because of what we did at our senior prom, or because that's what we've heard happens at senior proms. And based upon that belief, we feel the fear, and then we think about our fear over and over, therefore producing worry. What we are really doing is supporting the exact thing we are worried about.

The question we should be asking ourselves is this: "Is the worry I'm experiencing supporting the safety and well-being of my teenager, or does my worry contribute to the problem?" To say it in another way, "Is what I'm feeling and thinking resourceful or nonresourceful? Does my worry 'restrict' my energy, or does it 'expand' it and allow it to flow freely?" Any time that we are not feeling resourceful about any given situation, it always, in some way, contributes to the problem. Of course the real problem it creates is inside us, in the form of a restriction of free-flowing energy. It then puts our focus on the restriction and sets the law of attraction in motion to bring back to us more of the same.

Worry, in itself, uses a lot of emotional and physical energy. In an attempt to recover our lost energy, we sometimes become addicted to the worry.

There are basically four steps toward eliminating worry.

1. Become aware of yourself worrying; then go to the next step and observe yourself worrying.
2. As you observe yourself worrying and feeling fearful, make the conscious effort to drop your thoughts about what you fear.
3. Embrace your fear. Observe yourself feeling fearful, and no matter how difficult it may be, allow your fear emotion to surface, and then let it go.

4. Let go of your need to be in control of an outcome over which you have no control.

Worry is a killer. It can lead to many types of addictions such as alcoholism, overeating, drug abuse and other escaping behaviors. What we are really doing when we worry is identifying with our fear so that we can escape from our pain. If we don't accept our feelings and allow the attached emotion to surface, we choose to suppress, repress or judge them as bad. By doing so, we resist experiencing the feeling, which in turn will allow it to resurface as some other worry at another time.

We have a choice about how we handle our feelings of fear. We can express them, suppress them, repress them or let them go. When we choose either of the first three, they will always be trapped inside, just waiting for the right time to surface again.

Letting Go of Our Expectations

When we bury unhappiness, we also bury the cause of our unhappiness. It's absolutely impossible to be truly happy and at the same time cling to unhappiness. As long as we are looking outward for answers to our happiness, we are not looking in the right direction. Only when we begin to observe and to comprehend all the processes of how we create our own suffering are we free to choose not to live with the suffering anymore. The only effective and final way to deal with nonresourceful feelings and emotions is to observe them and let them go.

Let's say we lose our job. Of course we may feel hurt, angry, betrayed and even fearful, unless, of course, we wanted to get a new job in the first place. In that case we may be relieved. We have a choice as to how long we want to hang on to our nonresourceful feelings about losing our job. As long as we are feeling nonresourceful about losing our job, being resourceful about finding a new one will be difficult. When we take action from a position of nonresourcefulness, it becomes impossible to allow resourceful solutions.

Feeling nonresourceful about losing our job is not a requirement. Letting go of the fear, anger, etc., that we feel about losing our job is not a requirement. It's simply a way to end the suffering about losing our job and to get on with finding another one. As long as we are clinging to any fixed thought or feeling about how our life or circumstances should be, we will always suffer to one degree or another. A great deal of the time, life just simply won't be the way we expect it to be. So we might as well just relax. We might as well let go. What have we got to lose? It just might work! And we certainly won't know until we try it.

The moment we let go of our expectations, everything changes, even if nothing external changed at all. The reason everything changed is that when we let go, we switch from a nonresourceful state to a resourceful one.

Consider for a moment where the change actually occurs

when we let go. The change occurred inside, and all we did was let go of our resistance. When we are always trying to make things be the way we want them to be, we become tense and we live in a state of resistance. We then come to a false conclusion: "We are in control." But that conclusion is only an illusion. If we observe ourselves closely, we'll discover that all we are really controlling is keeping our non-resourceful feelings in place by hanging on to our fears. When we hang on we are keeping new solutions out of sight. When we let go, only then are we free of the pain that our own resistance has created.

Absolutely nothing can take our peace of mind away from us. We have to voluntarily give it up! And we give it up so easily, and for just about anything—red lights, people's opinions, traffic, old hurts, things not going our way, etc.

Here's a four-step formula for discovering and handling nonresourceful feelings in your life:

1. Take a look at what you are experiencing as an obstacle in your life, in your business, relationship, family or personally.
2. What belief are you clinging to about how life should be that creates your own obstacles?
3. What do you have to gain by having this obstacle in your life? What do you have to gain by not having this obstacle in your life? Take some time and make a list of what you have to gain by having it, and a list of what

you have to gain by not having it. Now, notice which list is longer.

4. What would happen if you let go of what you believe you have to gain by keeping this obstacle in your life?

A few years ago in one of my workshops in Phoenix, I led a woman through the above process. I asked for someone who had a goal that they wanted to share. She said that her goal was to lose 180 pounds and that she had been on every diet imaginable, about thirty total. At that time she weighed about 300 pounds. I began asking her two questions as I listed her answers on a chart, which I had split down the middle. I started by asking her what she had to gain by losing the weight? The first response was that she would look better. Then I asked her what she had to gain by keeping the weight on, to which she answered, "Nothing." I again asked her what she had to gain by losing the weight, and she responded by saying that she would feel better. Then I asked again what she had to gain by keeping the weight, and again she responded by answering, "Nothing." We continued with the questions until we had completely filled several pages on the left side with what she had to gain by losing the weight. On the right side under what she had to gain by keeping it, we hadn't written a thing.

Again I asked her what she had to gain by keeping the weight. She hesitated for a few moments. I asked her again. Finally, with a great deal of difficulty, she answered, "I wouldn't have to have men touching me." Her next answer was, "I wouldn't have to commit to a relationship." Then she said, "I have something very difficult that I want to tell about." She said this was something that she had never told a soul. She went on to tell about one night twenty years ago when she was thirteen years old. She was the school football queen. One night after the game, she was walking home alone and was attacked and raped by four boys. She went home that night and vowed never to tell a soul. She also made a commitment right then that she would never, for the rest of her life, ever let a man touch her again. Then she began to eat, and eat, and eat, until she had gained more than 180 pounds, which she thought would protect her from men. Within about twenty minutes of working with her, she let go of her anger, her fears and her resentment once and for all.

Remember, she had been involved in more than thirty diet programs over the years without any success at all. Within six months, and only by letting go of a present emotion created from a past experience, she had lost eighty pounds without dieting. Over the next year she had lost 180 pounds, and all she did was let it go. She let go of her resistance to losing weight. She let go of her present resentment, which had been created by a past experience that she was hanging on to. By letting go of her present feeling about the past, she was in effect, healing the past.

Try this concept on a few of your obstacles that are keeping you from reaching your goals. See if you can discover what you have to gain by not having your goal, and what you have to gain by having it.

Energy in Motion

Let's look at our emotions. Emotions are the result of feelings that are being filtered through outdated beliefs. Let's say that we are feeling tired. That's a pure feeling. However, we may believe that we should not be tired. That's a belief. Because of the fact that we believe that we should not be tired, we now get depressed. The stronger the emotion, the stronger the underlying belief system.

The emotions that we most want to avoid, that keep us connected to and supporting our fears, are as follows:

Hopelessness: This emotion leads to a feeling of being "stuck." Hopelessness is almost a nonfeeling state. We feel stuck, restricted and immobilized. Oftentimes you may see this state with people living on the street. Even though there may be jobs all around, they can't see them. Why? Because when one is locked in hopelessness it's almost impossible to see the truth of their situation. We see and experience life only as we project. By projecting hopelessness, we are attracting more of the same. Hopelessness does not attract hope. Purpose is the only thing that eliminates hopelessness.

Sadness: An emotion that leads to loneliness and depression, tenses our bodies and holds us inward. In this state, our energy begins to move, but we still feel a restricted energy flow.

Fear: This emotion tenses our bodies and holds us back. It's a state of reliving the past in the present moment. Courage lets you move past fear. Fear is of the head. Courage is of the heart.

Anger: An emotion that tenses our bodies and pushes us forward. Anger is usually brought on by an extreme need for approval even though it appears to be a need to be in control. The person has a need to be right; therefore, they have a need to control their surroundings, knowing that by being right they receive the approval of others, or more accurately approval of themselves.

Ego–centered pride: An emotion that tenses our bodies and leads to anxiety, which is a combination of fear that holds us back, anger that pushes us forward, and depression that holds us inward. With anxiety we are pushing forward, pulling back and holding inward all at the same time. You can see why we don't really get anywhere in a state of anxiety. We are going so fast in all directions at the same time, hoping that when we arrive at our destination we can finally slow down. What never really occurs to us, because we are in such a panic with so much to do, is that what we really need to do is simply stop! We need to stop believing that our maze is actually leading us somewhere.

Ask yourself these two questions: How do you feel when you attempt to slow down, try to relax, or when you take a day or two off? Second, how do you keep yourself from relaxing, slowing down or taking time off?

Might as well relax a bit. Being the fastest person in a maze doesn't get us anywhere any faster. Besides, there is really nothing to prove, win or get anyway. We are all entered in the race of life, and in the end, we'll discover that we were just racing against ourselves. When we truly look at it, there is really no destination at all! So why not just relax now and then?

Each emotional state has its own frequency. In other words, it puts out a certain signal. When we're in that state we resonate with that frequency, therefore attracting more of the same. For example, hopelessness has a much lower frequency than, let's say, anger or fear. Hopelessness carries a more stuck type of energy, and a person who is stuck in hopelessness feels immobilized. If we are around this type of person for a period of time we may begin to feel or resonate, to some degree, the same way, or we'll feel that we want to get away from it or to help to change it. Hopelessness doesn't feel good, and unless we are totally absorbed by it, we want to get out of it as soon as possible. Once we become totally absorbed in it, we become trapped, feeling that there is no way out. And not only that, we'll stay there until we are acted upon by an outside force causing us to change.

Let's look at the emotional state, or vibration, of anger. Think of a time when you were in a playful or a peaceful mood, and suddenly you came in contact with someone who was angry. They might have been angry with you, or it might not have even been about you at all. Either way, how did you feel being around that person? You could feel that downward pull, couldn't you? The reason is that they are giving off a frequency of anger, which doesn't resonate with your feeling or field of peace or playfulness. It's like two channels coming in on the same radio station. Either one signal is stronger than the other, pushing the other out, or there is a sound of static and confusion. The same thing is going on inside us as well when we're around people who aren't on our frequency, who don't resonate with our frequency.

Feelings Create Emotions

Emotions are the effect of how we feel. In other words, feelings create emotions. Notice if any of the following words or phrases resonate with you. Keep in mind that we have a tendency to go in and out of various emotions, based upon how we feel at a given time. One minute we might be in a state of hopelessness, and the next moment we might be in a state of anger because of someone we come in contact with, and then the next moment we might find ourselves in a peaceful state because of a song we just heard.

Have you ever found yourself experiencing any of the following emotions? I can't. Failure. I give up. What's the use?

Can't win. Confused. Feeling stuck. Worthlessness. Nobody loves me. Nobody cares about me. I feel helpless.

These are emotions of hopelessness. If a person is in this state, what frequency are they are putting out to the world? That's exactly how they will perceive the world around them. If they project hopelessness, their world becomes hopeless. I'm sure that we wouldn't want to hang around a person who was feeling that way, at least not for very long. Why? Because we don't like how it feels, and we don't want to let them pull us down.

Say the word *hopeless.* Say it again. *Hopeless.* How does that make you feel when you say it? *Hopeless.* It doesn't feel very good, does it?

How does a person get into a hopeless state? We all do it. It's just that some stay there longer than others. A person can get there a little at a time, or it can happen all at once. Even when it seems to happen all at once, there were probably underlying issues that have been building up over a long period of time.

In a small town where I lived for a while, there was a man who lived inside a drainpipe at the edge of town. He never bothered anyone. He would hang around one of the restaurants where people would give him food and money to live. Everyone seemed to know him. One day I asked someone about where he came from and who he was. What I discovered was startling. It seems that he was once a stockbroker, with a seat on the New York Stock Exchange. One day he lost it all. The pressure was so great that in a day's time he went from a seat on the stock exchange to a seat in a drain-pipe. He went from having it all to hopelessness, and there he stayed until he died a few years later. He was killed by his own self-created hopelessness. In other words, he died from a disease called "hopelessness." Our human body is very loyal. It will even die for us if we tell it to do so. The truth is, we kill ourselves every day by what we are hanging on to that keeps us from living fully. It's not what happens to us that matters, it's how we handle what happens to us that makes the difference.

Let's move up the emotional frequency scale a bit to a higher frequency. Notice how you feel as you read the following words or phrases: *It's not fair. I feel lost. Why does this always happen to me? I feel unhappy. I feel hurt. I am disappointed. Self-pity. I feel guilty.*

How do these emotions make you feel? Maybe a little better than hopelessness, but still not very good? These feelings produce an emotional state of sadness, which is actually a higher-frequency emotion than hopelessness. Sadness has more movement, more feeling than hopelessness. It's less "stuck."

Say the word *sadness.* How does that make you feel? Say the word *disappointed.* Does that make you feel sad? Does feeling sad make you feel disappointed with life?

Moving up the emotional-frequency scale even higher, listen as you say these words out loud. Notice how they make you feel. Notice the energy they produce inside you:

I am worried. I feel afraid. I feel defensive. I am frustrated. There's never enough. I feel insecure.

What emotion do you feel? It is the emotional frequency of fear. Have you ever felt worried or afraid that something was not going to work out the way you wanted it to? In fact, all emotions are really based in fear, they are just disguised as something else. Hopelessness is really the ultimate state of fear. In hopelessness we fear even moving. We've been beaten down so many times that we just don't have the will to try again. We fear taking any action at all. Hopelessness is the ultimate fear of failing as well as the fear of living. We are so fearful that we become immobilized. Our energy is stuck.

Moving up the emotional-frequency scale again, see if you can identify with any of these emotions:

I want it done now!
Why don't you ever listen?
It's my way or no way.
I am jealous.

What do you think? *Anger.* We've probably all experienced this one at one time or another. *Impatience.* Feel yourself feeling impatient. Can you see the anger behind the feeling of impatience? Can you see how the feeling of impatience creates the emotional frequency of anger?

Now let's move on up to the top of the nonresourceful emotional-frequency scale. This is where we find a great deal of those we believe to be high achievers. See if you can identify with any of these:

Being judgmental
Being selfish
Being snobbish
Being a know-it-all
Being rigid
Being narrow-minded
Being opinionated
Being resistant to input
Being vain

This is the emotional frequency of ego-centered pride.

Look at me!
Look what I did!
Look what I accomplished!
I need no help from a higher power or anyone else!
I can do it myself!
Who needs resourcefulness, love, etc.?
I can accomplish anything all by myself.

This frequency creates a lot of movement, burns a lot of energy, and creates a lot of undue stress and heart attacks. From this emotional place, we are always in pursuit and never satisfied with the results we produce or what we have.

No matter how much it is, we always want more. We want life to be more. We want to have more fun. We want to make more money. When we get this or that, then we'll be happy. The problem is, we never get enough, because enough is never enough. There will always be more to get when living in this emotional state.

So it goes, up the emotional-frequency scale: hopelessness, sadness, fear, anger, ego-centered pride. Begin to notice when you are in these states. Begin to notice what it feels like to feel sad or angry, or when fear is holding you back. Begin to notice how you can observe yourself in a state of sadness. Begin to notice how these emotional frequencies keep you away from happiness and experiencing more self-love.

Letting go of an emotion such as anger is far more effective than letting go of a single feeling. You can let go of your impatient feeling, but when you let go of anger, you not only release your anger, but your impatience will be weakened, along with all the other connecting nonresourceful feelings. The emotion is what holds the feelings in place if not dealt with at the time it arises. When we let go of an emotion like anger, we are literally dumping or unraveling and disconnecting a tremendous number of feelings that are keeping the emotion alive.

Can you now begin to see why just changing our thinking won't do it? Thinking will not change a belief. There's a lot more involved than just positive thinking. We have to let go of the feeling or emotion that holds the belief in place.

The emotion is not the problem, as you might think. The emotion is the result. The emotion is the solution, if we observe it and let it go. Look at it this way: the emotion is just the tip of the iceberg. Ninety percent is still under the water in the form of trapped energy or feelings. As we begin to observe and let go of the emotion, the submerged portion begins to move into the light of observation and will begin to melt away as well. Each emotion is connected to feelings, and at the same time, feelings are connected to each other. So when we let go of one feeling, we will also be releasing many connecting feelings at the same time, or at least bringing them to the surface for observation and release.

A few years ago a man in one of my workshops was having a problem getting in touch with his feelings. Every time we would participate in a visualization exercise that was supposed to get him to feel, following it he would say that he felt nothing. I tried several approaches to break through and get him in touch with his feelings. Nothing worked. I had promised him that that we would break through before the two days ended. Finally, thirty minutes before the workshop ended, during the final exercise, he had a glimpse of a feeling he had experienced from some time in his past.

About three days later, I received a panic call from him claiming that his whole life was in shambles since the workshop. He said that he was having some problems in his relationship, that he was upset about the fact that someone had taken him for a large sum of money, and other things. I asked him how he felt. He said that he felt hurt, angry and betrayed. I said, "So, you are feeling?" I explained what was happening. By letting go of one feeling, a multitude of connecting feelings began to surface as well with which he needed to deal. He explained that the first release felt like a small hole being poked in a huge dam, and now he felt like the whole dam had broken.

Can you see the incredible value of letting go of an emotion such as fear or anger? The emotion is connected to all the feelings that are holding the emotion in place. At the same time, each feeling is connecting and supporting other feelings, holding them in place. Breaking the dam of feelings and emotions is absolutely the best thing that can happen to you, as long as you understand the nature of feelings and emotions and how to deal with them at a core level.

The Ego Is Your Friend

All our emotions are derived from past experiences. The sum total of our experiences forms our ego, or our personality. Someone once asked me what the purpose of our ego is. "Well," I said, "its real purpose is to create problems so that we will pay attention to what it is we need to let go of in order to move forward and get rid of our ego." Actually our ego is our greatest ally; it is a problem solver if you understand it. It provides an awesome opportunity for growth. Look at your ego as your assistant. Every time it brings up a problem, what it's doing is offering you a perfectly planned opportunity to let go, resolve an old issue and grow.

Our greatest power, the release of our authentic power, will come from the understanding that we do not have to respond to any voices or disturbances within us. When we feel any emotion—fear, anger, etc.—just know that the proper use of that emotion is simply to get the message, then to turn off the alarm clock by observing it and then letting it go. When we feel any emotion, such as fear, what it is there for is to get us to realize just exactly what it is we are frightened of in the first place. Once you see the truth, see exactly what it is you are frightened of, you can now resign yourself to it, should it really happen. This will also turn off your fear alarm. It's also really important to know not to take any steps to resolve your fear until you've turned off your fear alarm. Taking any steps without first turning off your alarm will actually strengthen and feed your fear, allowing it to return at a later time with more strength.

When we feel anger, the purpose is to get us to realize just what it is we are attached to, and afraid of losing, that's causing us to feel angry. The first step is to turn off your anger alarm by observing it and then letting it go; then take the necessary steps needed to minimize the loss. If we take steps before turning off our alarm, we will be taking action from a place of nonresourcefulness, and producing more of the very thing we are trying so hard to get rid of in the first place.

There is a caution we should take when experiencing

anger. It is really easy to get caught in the trap of blaming others for our anger. What really happens in a blameful attack is not only that we are hurting the other person, but we are also being hurt in the process. An angry person will eventually end up destroying themselves if they become too vindictive. Blaming others for our anger may seem easier at the time than letting go and being nonreactive, but what's really happening is that we are just avoiding facing our own feelings. The end result of this kind of action is further suppression of our feelings. Suppression is always the real motive behind expressing our anger. Our anger is always brought about by our fear of what we might lose, whereas sadness is always over what we fear we have lost. So we can see that both sadness and anger, or any other nonresourceful emotion, is always fear-based. All of these emotions should be considered our greatest gifts, because they are truly based in love. Every time we experience a nonresourceful emotion of any kind, it is being given to us by love as an opportunity for self-discovery, self-healing and personal growth.

It's truly important to know why we experience emotions the way we do. Anger, for example, is just energy, although it is a different form of energy than sadness or hopelessness. Why? The reason it's different is that we have labeled it differently. It's the same energy, only with a different label. Just like my pen on my desk and the paper I write on are different forms of the same energy. When we begin to see each of our feelings or emotions as just energy—without labels, judgments or evaluations—we remove their importance, and we are left with just energy. Look at it this way. A feeling without a self-created label of any kind is hardly something we should be frightened of in any way, is it? In fact, without the self-created label we place on our feelings, there is no feeling at all. So, there is absolutely no reason to resist any feeling, because it's just energy coming up to be released back into usable energy once again.

The letting-go process is not about using effort, willpower or our brain to change one thing into another, like trying to turn a negative into a positive. When we begin to see our feelings and emotions for what they really are, only energy, we'll then realize that neither positive nor negative exist, they are just more self-created labels designed to further suppress our painful feelings.

Letting go should be an effortless process. Hanging on is what uses up all our energies and causes us so much pain. Letting go requires no effort at all. It's more of a choice. Letting go is simply a process of releasing restrictive energy, and then enjoying the flow of resourceful loving energy—our authentic power—and self-love once again. By simply observing the feeling as it is, which is just self-labeled, trapped energy, the experience basically transmutes itself. There is no effort involved at all with letting go, only choice: the choice both to become self-observant and to let go. Together they yield self-discovery and personal transformation. Letting go is as simple as the statement "Wow, what a relief!"

7

Letting Go of the Need for Control

*We get hurt not by
what others say
or do, but rather by
our own need to control
how others act toward us.
When we let go of our
demands, people can
act as they wish and
we can remain at peace*

T he greatest human need is the need to feel needed, wanted and loved. How we communicate, what we say, how we dress and walk, our smile, the words we use, our need to control others . . . all these stem either directly or indirectly from our need to be accepted and loved.

As small children we felt the need to be accepted, loved and connected to our parents. The need is so strong and so much a part of us that we carry it with us all our lives. As we grow into our childhood and teen years, we feel a need to be accepted by our peers. Next we begin to look for acceptance from those with whom we work. And as we become parents ourselves, we want to be accepted by our children, wanting them to love us and to remain connected.

In our attempt to stay connected, we experience two basic emotions: love and fear. There are many ways, however, that we express or act out these emotions.

To repeat, fear is taking a past experience, projecting it into the future—with the anticipation of it happening again—and then reliving it in the present. As we have previously discussed, we may express our fears in many ways. For example, we may experience it as hopelessness, fearing that we are lost and there is no way out. In this state we feel stuck and are afraid to move. We may express our fear as sadness when we have to live without something or someone we have lost. We may express our fear in the form of fear itself. Fear restricts our energy and holds us back. Fear usually comes from not wanting to repeat a mistake. Anger is another way we express our fears. When we are in a state of anger, we fear what we may lose. The last way we experience our fears is when we are operating from a place of self-centered pride. In this state, we feel that there is never enough and that we must always be working toward having more, toward keeping up with the Joneses.

Feelings Are Stored in the Body

As a result of all our past experiences, we have literally millions of stored feelings, or trapped energy patterns, all of which resonate at different frequencies. We sort our feelings into individual frequency categories that become emotions. All nonresourceful emotions can be labeled as fear, even though they may appear in our lives as hopelessness, sadness, fear, anger or self-centered pride. These emotions have been created by a past experience that made us feel hopeless or angry, or by reliving a past experience over and over again. We then begin to act out in our everyday lives the need to be accepted. We may also act them out as our need to be in control. However, our need to be in control, we'll discover with close observation, is really a disguise for our need to be accepted.

Which came first? Was it the feeling, the emotion or our need to be accepted? The experience came first. We then trap the energy of the experience inside in the form of a feeling. The feeling comes to the surface in the form of an emotion to be released. We then have a choice to either re-experience it and let it go or to suppress it, making it even stronger for a later appearance. The more we suppress, the stronger our need to feel connected or accepted. Out of our deep need to let go of the feeling and emotion and reconnect to our own true nature, we begin to act out our feelings in two behavior patterns. The first is our need to be accepted, and the other is our need to be in control, which is really our underlying need to be accepted. Acceptance is always the dominant need we all have.

The need to be accepted results from the repeated suppression of the emotion as it comes up to be released. The need to be in control is how we attempt to keep the emotion suppressed, the feeling buried and to force others to be accepting of us.

A *need* is defined as "a situation of great difficulty or misfortune." *Need* is the key word. When we are in a state of need for anything, we are automatically in a state of difficulty. As we discussed earlier, *need* has the same meaning as *lack*. When we focus on lack, we are always in a state of nonresourcefulness. We are in a state of need or lack. So when we need control, we are lacking control, and when we need acceptance, we have none.

You may be asking yourself, *How can I be in control, without needing to be in control? And, if I let go of control, won't I then be out of control?* We don't let go of control; we only let go of our need to be in control, as well as our underlying need to be accepted. None of us has any control over what happens to us next or what others might think of us or decisions someone else might make. When we let go of our need to know what's going to happen next, or what others may think of us, we are letting go of our attachment, our expectation of the outcome. If we live our lives trying to second-guess what's going to happen or being upset when things aren't going our way or worrying about what others might think of us, we are living our lives in a state of nonresource-fulness or difficulty. The real questions we want to ask ourselves are, "Does this support my vision of the desired outcome I want to produce in my life, or does it distract? Does it restrict my energy or does it expand it? Does it provide me with a solution, or keep me away from seeing a solution? Does it let me live resistance-free, or does it contribute to my stress?"

Let's say that I wanted to raise some capital to start a new business. I have my business plan in place, and I'm ready to present my project to some investors. Suddenly I begin to doubt my ability to raise the needed capital. The questions I should be asking myself are: "Is my feeling of doubt moving me closer to raising my capital or further away? Am I contributing to the solution or to the problem? Is my feeling of doubt a need for acceptance or a need for control?"

All our nonresourceful thoughts, words, feelings, emotions and behaviors are derived from the need for acceptance and the need to be in control, which is just the need to be accepted in disguise. When we begin to let go of these two needs, we'll also discover that fear-based emotions such as hopelessness, sadness, fear, anger and ego-centered pride, as well as the connecting feelings holding them in place, will all begin to wither away from lack of attention.

For many, out of their fear of being alone, the need to be accepted has become their life-support system. We seek acceptance, so that we can have more people around us. We seek control, so that we have influence over others, therefore having more people around us, so that we can gain greater acceptance. The reality is that the more we seek acceptance or control, the less we actually have in our lives.

A need-to-be-accepted behavior suppresses the emotion that supports the feelings that support the beliefs that influence behavior that produces the result which in turn support the need to be accepted. The need to be accepted is really our overriding behavior that keeps all our emotions and feelings suppressed.

Basically, the phenomenon begins with the experience. The experience traps the feeling energy. Next comes the belief. We begin to believe that the energy we've trapped inside is who we are. Next, in order to get back to our natural state of happiness and joy, the emotion is triggered by some new experience that reminds us of an old experience. If the emotion is released, we move forward with our growth. If the emotion is suppressed because we don't want to deal with it, the original experience is now enhanced and made stronger. In order to keep the emotion suppressed, our need-to-control behavior comes forth, really arising from our need to be accepted. All this stems from our underlying need to once again know and love ourselves.

To better understand the need to be in control and the need for acceptance, let's separate the two. Let's first discuss the need to be in control as it relates to the need to be accepted, and how these needs came into existence. If we look back over our lives, we could probably come up with a long list of people who hurt us in some way. We all have our list. The parent, the schoolteacher, the husband, the wife, the child, the best friend . . . the list is endless. Because of our catalog of hurts and pains, we develop patterns of avoidance that cause us to develop a conditioned way of thinking and perceiving life. We develop these behavior patterns of avoidance by trying so desperately to avoid our own self-created pain.

The Need to Be in Control

We begin to judge others. We judge ourselves. We form opinions about anyone or anything that we fear might cause us any sort of pain. Most of us spend our whole lives attempting to move in a direction that keeps us from any discomfort. We believe we are victims, so we attempt to arrange our whole life to be in control. But without realizing it what we are really doing is setting up a life that is out of control. We have become so obsessed with not being hurt and remaining in control, our real life passes us by without our noticing it. We spend 90 percent of our time defending our needs.

Our methods for avoiding pain have become almost endless. When we are threatened in any way, we instantly react by putting up a barrier of some sort that we hope will keep us in control. But in reality, what is really happening is that we are clouding our vision by our need to control. Because most of us are in a reactive state every few minutes, or even seconds, our vision of how we want our lives to be or how life really is is completely out of focus. We become caught up in the dramas that we've set up to protect ourselves, to keep us feeling in control, when in reality we are getting further out of control all the time.

Let's say that we have an idea or a belief of how something should be. For example, we want our house to be absolutely spotless all the time. With this in mind, we are always looking for ways to clean the house. There's nothing wrong with wanting to keep a clean home, but let's say that we have a family with four children under the age of twelve. The belief "I need to have a spotless home all the time" produces a behavior derived from the need to be in control instead of a behavior stemming from a real need. If we have four children who are under twelve, our home is realistically not going to be spotless all the time, unless, of course, we place a great deal more importance on having a spotless home than on our family. This is called the need to control. "My home must be clean all the time. Homes should be clean, no matter what."

If we believe that it is bad for our house to not be clean, this is known as a control drama. If we are concerned about what others will think of us if our house isn't clean, this is known as an acceptance drama. Most of the time, the two work hand in hand. We want to be in control so that we can gain acceptance from others. We may not even be seeking acceptance from those in our lives today. We may be seeking acceptance from one of our parents who had a control drama going on when we were children. Maybe our life felt as if it were out of control back then. As a result we feel we need to regain the control we feel we lost sometime along the way.

The way to begin to release our concerns about having to have a spotless home is by letting go of the need to be in control all the time. The key is to learn to identify those things we can control from those we cannot. In other words, to learn to identify the difference between controllable and uncontrollable circumstances.

Any circumstance that is beyond our control is not our responsibility. If, however, there is an action that should be taken, we should first let go of our need to control the outcome, then take action. By doing so, we truly remain in control. We remain in control of our thoughts, feelings, emotions and behaviors, which is the only thing we really have control of in the first place. If there is no action that we can take at the time, we should simply let go of our need to control and have the courage to leave it at that.

Concerning ourselves over having a clean house, or what others think, or about how something should turn out, is a nonresourceful leak of our resourceful energy. Whatever happens that is beyond our control should simply be accepted as a necessary part of the overall process. A seemingly nonresourceful event just may be taking place for the purpose of keeping us in a certain place long enough for the real event to happen, or to give us the opportunity to let go of our need for control, or both.

When we let go of the need to control, we don't actually give up control at all, or give up using any of our skills. What we really give up is using our skills to manipulate the world and the people in our lives, trying to make them the way we would like them to be.

When *We* Change, Those Around Us Change

A woman in one of my workshops was having difficulty with her seventeen-year-old son. She said that he had become totally uncontrollable. He was on drugs and alcohol and in the habit of coming home high, that is, when he came home at all. He had the habit of staying out until three or four o'clock in the morning and never called. Sometimes he would stay out for two and three days at a time. She explained that they were always in some sort of a battle about his behavior. She attempted to get him involved in a drug and alcohol rehabilitation program, with no luck at all.

One day, she had had all that she could take of the situation, so she joined a Tough Love group. Tough Love recommends telling your child that you really love him, but you can no longer tolerate his behavior, and that he can no longer live in your home. She basically locked him out of the house.

The next step for the mother was to attend support meetings two times a week to help her handle the guilt she was feeling for abandoning her son. I asked her how she felt about the situation and about her son. She said that she felt very guilty about what she was doing to her son, and at the same time she felt very angry toward him for his behavior. She said, "I just want him to stop. I just want us to love each other again."

I asked her what she was feeling. She said that she felt angry and frustrated. I asked her if she felt that her anger and frustration came from a need to be in control or a need for acceptance. She said she thought it was her need to be in control. I asked if she would mind answering some questions. She agreed.

I asked her if she liked feeling the way she did. Looking a little perplexed that I had asked such a question, she answered, "No, of course I don't."

I next asked her, "Do you want to let it go?" To which she answered, "Yes, I do."

My next question was, "Are you willing to let go of your need to control your son?" She answered hesitantly, "I think so."

I asked her once again, "Are you willing to let go of your need to be in control?" She said, "I'm afraid to say yes."

Once again I asked, "Are you willing to let it go?" With some hesitation, she finally answered, "Yes, I am."

The last question I asked her was, "When? When are you willing to let it go?" She said, "Maybe a little later, or tomorrow?"

Again I asked, "When are you willing to let go of your need to be in control?" She breathed a big sigh of relief as she answered, *"Now."*

After processing her feelings about the situation several times in different ways, and recognizing her need to control her son's behavior, she discovered that the most important thing she could do for her son was to stay in a resourceful and happy state. After we worked together some more, and as she gained a deeper understanding of the part she played in the situation, she completely let go of her need to be in control of her son's behavior. She simply let go of her need to control something that was beyond her ability to control.

A short time after the workshop, she called me to share her good news. Her son had moved back into the house. He joined a drug and alcohol rehab program. He started coming in before midnight, and if he was going to be late, he called to let her know where he was. And to top it off, he had joined the Peace Corps.

She said earlier that day she had sat down with him for a heart-to-heart talk. She asked him why he had changed so quickly. He told her that he hadn't changed at all, that she was the one who had made a change.

Her son wanted to simply be in charge of his own life, and she wanted to be in control of his every action. All she did was to let go of her need to control him, and when she changed as a result, then he began to change, and very quickly. When we hang on to our need to control, we create resistance. Remember, we see and experience in life only what we are projecting.

The Invisible Connection

When we need to control another person, we have set up an invisible, nonresourceful, emotional connection between ourself and that person. This energy connection is what I call a *chain of pain,* a chain that never gets broken until someone lets go. If we are feeling angry toward another person, not only is our anger having an adverse effect on us, but it is also having a similar effect on the other person as well, even though we may not be verbally expressing it. One feeling of anger toward another can and does sometimes affect hundreds of people we don't even know. The way this works is that we are holding anger, or any other nonresourceful feeling, and someone else feels our feeling, which in turn lowers their resourceful energy pattern, or vibrational frequency, and so on, as both of us come in contact with others. So we could look at it this way. When we let go, we are breaking a chain of pain, a chain that may be connected and may reach completely around the world. If we can begin to see how every act of violence could spread in this way, it's not hard to see why so many conflicts exist on the planet.

Any Action That Is Not Love Is an Act of Violence

Violence comes in a lot of packages. Anger, for example, is violence. Not being considerate of another is an act of violence. Disciplining a child while in an angry state is an act of violence. Any action toward another that is not love is, to one degree or another, an act of violence. Imagine this scenario. Two world leaders get upset with one another, and out of that upset, there's some sort of political conflict that needs to. As it progresses, they begin to threaten one another. A small armed conflict breaks out. Now the allies of each country decide to get involved. We send troops to help stop the conflict, but it accelerates into a full-scale war. Some of our troops are killed in the process. Then the families of the soldiers who were killed get angry and begin to express their anger to others. The news media get involved and accelerate the problem even more. Angry protestors demonstrate to stop the war, which in turn upsets the police, who get angry and begin fighting the people who only wanted peace in the first place. We can begin to see why it is vitally important for each of us to take responsibility for letting go of needing control, for remaining resourceful and then for taking action from that place, instead of becoming a part of the ongoing drama, the chain of pain.

Letting go of the need to control is like sailing, surfing, skiing or living life to the fullest. It requires a subtle blend of control, with the help of skill and knowledge, and going with the flow. Letting go of our need to control simply means letting go of our attachment to the outcome. Anything we cling to will eventually cause us pain. When we are in pain, we set up a chain of pain.

When we discipline a child our tendency is to demand that they act a certain way. What would happen if you demanded that your friend across the street acted a certain way? They would probably tell you where to get off! When we demand, we push the resistance button of the other person, whether our friend, our children or whoever. The resistance we encounter in turn pushes our need-to-be-in-control button, escalating the matter into a full-scale argument, until someone decides to let go and break the chain of pain. Letting go of your need to control allows you to live resistance-free.

When we make demands of our children, we raise demanding children. On the other hand, when we let go of our need to control them, we are coming from a nonviolent, loving place, where we begin to connect heart-to-heart. On the one hand we could say, "Go clean your room. It looks like a pigpen. Don't you have any pride at all?" On the other hand we could connect heart-to-heart by saying, "Your room looks a little messy. Would you mind giving it a good cleaning today? It makes me feel really good when you have a clean room."

The most important thing in the world to each of us should be to maintain our own peace of mind, our own happiness. It's more important than your mate's happiness, your children's happiness or your family's happiness. Why? Taking action from a resourceful, happy state of mind is the key to making a difference, or breaking the chain of pain, because resourceful thinking and feeling lead to resourceful actions, and resourceful actions lead to resourceful solutions. On the other hand, taking action from a place of non-resourcefulness only leads to nonresourceful solutions, or no solutions at all.

Get Clear About What You Want and Don't Want

I was having dinner one night with a networking club. Everyone at the table was sharing their goals and visions for their life's work. When it came time for the woman next to me to share, she said that she was very upset because she didn't have a vision for her life's work. She said that everyone told her she needed to clarify her vision and find some meaningful project to work on. I asked her what she wanted to do, and she said that all she knew was she wanted to make a difference for others, but she didn't know what that would look like. I asked her how the rest of her life was going. She said that she was very happy. She explained that she was financially secure, she had a good relationship with her husband and that basically everything in her life was great, except for not knowing what she could do to contribute to the lives of others.

I then asked her how she felt about not having a clear vision about how she might make a contribution. She answered, "Frustrated and a little depressed." I asked her if her frustration could be categorized as a need to control or a need for acceptance. She said she thought it was her need to control as well as her need to find some work that would make a contribution. I then asked if her depression and her need to be in control were contributing to anyone else's life. She said, "No, I don't think it is." I asked if her being satisfied and happy with the other areas of her life made a contribution to others, to which she answered, "Yes, I believe I set a good example for others to follow."

By letting go of her need to control the situation of not having a vision of how to make a contribution, her frustration went away and with it her problem. She could now make a contribution to everyone she came in contact with by the example she set. A short time after that, in fact that night during dinner, she discovered what she could do to make a significant difference in the lives of millions of people.

All she really needed to do was to create a vision of wanting to know what her vision was, let go of her fear and frustration of not knowing, and then simply have the courage to leave it at that and see what appears.

When we're stuck in a state of nonresourcefulness or frustration, there is no room for the right solution to come forth. We simply continue to attract more of the same. By letting go and returning to re-"source"-ful-ness, we return to source, where all things originate.

Conflicts, inner as well as outer, can always be resolved for the good of all involved if the first step is letting go of our need to control the outcome. When we approach a situation wanting to be in total control of the outcome, we don't allow for healing and true growth to take place, because our solution is based on what we want, not necessarily what is best for all involved. Just like in an argument, our solution is almost always based on what we want, not necessarily what is best. In an argument, we get so caught up in our need to be in control, in our need to be right, in our underlying need to be accepted as being right, that we can't recognize a resourceful solution even if one comes along. But when we let go of all our attachments to the outcome, the appropriate solution will always appear. What really happens when we let go of our need to control is that we make room for the appropriate solutions to come forth. As long as we are hanging on, we continue to suppress the nonresourceful emotion, and there's no room for solutions, just the rehashing of old problems.

What You Try to Control, Controls You

Let's explore some of the ways that we may use the need to be in control in our everyday lives. As you go through the list, note the ones with which you identify:

Not forgiving someone and holding grudges for past mistakes

Being prejudiced and thinking that you are better than others

Rejecting others to make yourself look good

Putting others down to make you look good

Getting even so that you feel in control

Being late just to show that you are in control

Being impatient to show others how important you are

Using manipulation to look better to others

Holding grudges in order to stay in control

Being rigid and doing it your way in order to take all the credit

Undermining others to make yourself look better

Always having strings attached in order to exercise your authority

Exercising aggressive behavior in order to be first or best

Judging others to make yourself look better

Saying "I'll try" so that you won't look bad if you don't follow through

Being a workaholic to show others how important you are

Blaming others to avoid seeing the truth

Let's review a few of these, and see how they can become a need to control.

Manipulation

To manipulate is defined as "to alter a situation to suit your own purpose." That about sums it up, doesn't it? Let's say you are in sales, and you're about to make an important call that you've been waiting on for months. It's a big account, one that you really want to acquire. So you plan and scheme and try to think of every tricky technique in the book to close the sale. You become obsessed, fearful and anxious about getting the account.

It's all right to plan, to be prepared, and to make an effective, well-organized presentation that leads to the sale. That's skill. But what doesn't work is being obsessed, fearful and anxious, wanting to control or manipulate the outcome of the presentation. What I'm suggesting is to let go of your need to control the outcome so that you can keep your attention on the presentation at hand. Remember that nonresourceful actions produce nonresourceful solutions. Beneath our need to control the outcome most likely lies our need to be accepted by our boss and peers.

Being Rigid

Another way we try to control is by being rigid about how to create a certain outcome. A few months ago, I was thinking that I would like to give some lectures at a local college. I asked a business associate if he knew how I might go about it or whom I might contact. He suggested that I call the college and ask. What a concept! So I wrote down in my day planner to do so the next day.

That evening, I stopped by my favorite health-food restaurant for dinner, where I sat at the counter to eat. A woman sat down next to me, said hello and asked me what I was having for dinner. We continued our conversation, sharing about what we did for work. As it turned out she was a professor in charge of the marketing department at the college where I wanted to speak. When she found out about my workshops she grew excited. She indicated that she would love to attend the next one in the area. But more than that, she said that she would like to invite me to be a guest speaker at the college for some of her students.

She was the perfect contact to facilitate my desire to speak at the college, wouldn't you agree? I couldn't have created that situation in a million years from a need to control. A clear vision is very powerful, as long as we don't place restrictions on how and when it will happen by being rigid. Here's a great saying to remember: Create your vision, and play with whoever shows up to play!

Create Your Vision and Leave It at That

A few years ago I was consulting for a seminar production company in Phoenix. I lived in Sedona, two hours away. The company contracted with me to assist them in hiring and training some instructors to teach their courses. I was thinking about who might be a good candidate for the job. I suddenly thought of a woman I knew in southern California named Mary Johnson. As I visualized Mary teaching this course, I thought that she would be perfect. My second thought was that I had lost touch and had no idea how to reach her. I instantly let it go and went back to seeing her teaching the course, thinking that I would somehow get in touch with her. I looked at my watch and it was 3:00 P.M. Remembering that I had to be in Sedona at 5:00 P.M. for my son's baseball game, I left for the day, not giving Mary another thought.

The next morning when I arrived at the office, a fax was lying on my desk:

To whom it may concern:

I am a graduate of your course from about eight months ago. I was very impacted by your program. I have a background in speaking and conducting workshops. Because of my background and the impact your program had on me, should the opportunity ever arise, I would like very much to be considered as one of your workshop leaders.

Sincerely,
Mary Johnson

I hardly believed that it could be the same Mary Johnson. I picked up the telephone and called the number on the fax, and to my surprise, it was the very same person! During the course of our conversation, I asked her exactly when she started thinking about contacting the company about becoming an instructor. She said, "Well, I was just sitting around yesterday thinking about what I wanted to do with my life. I felt a desire to make a change. Then suddenly, I began thinking about the workshop that I attended several months before, and how much of an impact it had on me. I thought, wouldn't it be great to be able to teach the course? So I sat down and wrote the letter and faxed it to the company." The next question, which I couldn't wait to ask, was, "What time was it when you wrote the letter?" Her reply was that she started thinking about it around 3:00 P.M. the day before, and faxed it around 5:00. You might call it a coincidence, but I call it being clear without the need to control the outcome.

Discipline with Love

Another great example of letting go of the need to be in control, instead of trying to be forceful in a situation was with my son Warren when he was around six years old. One day I was just walking out the front door of my house when I saw Warren running across the street to retrieve the mail from the mailbox. In his excitement to get there, he didn't take the time to look for cars before crossing the street. And just as he made it to the other side, a car traveling at a pretty good speed just missed him by inches. It was sort of a blind hill. He didn't look for the car, and the driver couldn't see him until he was right on him.

You can imagine how I felt. I was experiencing a combination of fear, relief and anger all at the same time. Once I saw that he was all right, I decided that there were two approaches I could take: to discipline him out of anger, or to correct the situation so that it never happened again.

Here's the first approach I could have taken. "Warren! Are you stupid or what! Didn't you see that car? You could have been killed! Are you too dumb to know to look before you cross the street? What if that car had run over you? Think about how your mother and I would have felt! How could you be so unconscious? Don't you ever do that again, you got it?"

Here's the approach I chose instead. I walked out to the street and said, "Hey, Warren, what are you doing?" He said, "I'm getting the mail for you and mom." And I said, "Do you have a minute?" Looking somewhat surprised, he said, "Sure, Dad, what for?" I said, "Why don't you come over here, and let's sit on the curb and talk. But, before you do, be sure to look both ways before you cross the street."

Our conversation went something like this. "Warren, do you see this street in front of us?" He said, "Yes." I said, "Do you know what the street is for?" He said, "Sure, Dad, it's for cars to drive on." Then I said, "Do you see that hill right there?" He said, "Yes." "You know, Warren, when cars come up over that hill, it's sometimes hard for them to see a little guy like you crossing the street." Then I said, "Do you know how much Mom and I love you? We love you a lot, and we wouldn't ever want anything to happen to you. So would you do Mom and me a big favor?" He said, "Yes, what do you want me to do?" "Well," I said, "the next time you come and get the mail, would you stop right here at the curb and look both ways for cars before you cross the street? And before you come back, do the same thing from the other side. Could you do that for Mom and me?" He said, "Sure, Dad. Can I go now?"

Which approach to the situation do you feel would be more effective—getting your point across from a place of

resourcefulness and love, or from a place of nonresourcefulness and anger? Would it have been better to satisfy my anger
and be right, and to make him wrong, or simply to *do* what's
right? Our children rebel against us because we push and
discipline instead of correct and love. Let go of the need to
be in control before taking action puts us in total control, or
at least as much control as is possible. When we are really in
control, we are in a state of love.

I'll Try

Referring back to our list, another method most of us use
to stay in control is using the phrase "I'll try." *I'll try* is
defined as "I'll struggle." When we say "I'll try," the other
person wants to believe that we have made a commitment to
them. But by saying "I'll try," we've committed only if what
we said we would try to do actually happens. If it doesn't
happen, we can point out that we said we would try, and we
did our best, but we just couldn't and we're really sorry. So
we're off the hook and still in control. But are we really in
control? The real question is how does the other person feel:
resourceful or nonresourceful? Remember that we have a
connection to that person. Remember the chain of pain?
Whether we are the sender or the recipient, we are involved.
Saying "I'll try" so that we don't have to commit is definitely
an act of violence toward the other person.

Blame

Possibly the most common controlling action is blame. Refraining from blame doesn't mean that we become incapable of knowing what is appropriate or inappropriate behavior in others. But when our energy is twisted and unfocused by always blaming, we become incapable of thinking, speaking and acting in a resourceful way in an effort to always appear right to others. We become literally blinded by our own blame toward the other person. Blame puts us into a nonresourceful state, where the real issues remain hidden.

Blaming is brought on by suppressed anger. When we are blaming, two things take place. First, we begin to look outside ourselves for the answers. We blame our circumstances or others for how we feel. Second, by blaming we suppress our anger even further. The act of blaming will keep our power outside us. It basically keeps us out of resourcefulness. When we blame, we see ourselves as victims who are powerless to make a change. Someone else is always doing something to us.

The blaming person thinks that everyone is out to get them. It is one of the ultimate control dramas. "My kids won't behave because they want me to suffer" is the ultimate control drama. The next time you catch yourself blaming, remember that the thing you feel you need to control actually controls you. When we allow ourselves to be controlled by outside circumstances, the controller, or the one who blames, only grows more afraid of losing control. In reality, the only thing we lose by letting go of our need to control is our self-created fear of not being in control, which was just imaginary control in the first place. What we really gain with blame is only the illusion of control, which comes from our fear of being out of control. Remember, that which we attempt to control actually controls us, and when we let go of the need to be in control, only then are we truly in control.

What always lies beneath our need to control is the need for acceptance. You might say that we only have one drama, an acceptance drama. I've only separated the two to make it easier to see exactly what we need to let go of.

When we always need acceptance from others, we are giving up our freedom. Wanting acceptance from others will lead us to actions that are based on what others want, not what we want. When we seek acceptance, we may find that we take actions in order to receive others' approval instead of taking action that we truly want to take. In other words, we may be doing something for someone else, and that's all right. But the real reason we are doing it is because they want us to do it, not because it is something we truly want to do.

Go over the following list of questions to see how much of a need for acceptance you may have:

1. You feel that you should give up your own interests in order to please others.

262 · L<small>ETTING</small> G<small>O</small> <small>OF THE</small> N<small>EED FOR</small> C<small>ONTROL</small>

2. You need the acceptance of others in order to feel good about yourself.

3. When someone strongly expects you to do something for them, you more often than not feel that you should do it.

4. You feel that your value as a person greatly depends upon what others think of you.

5. If someone dislikes you, you feel less worthwhile.

6. If someone disagrees with you, you generally take it personally.

7. Before you confront someone about a sensitive issue, you begin to imagine all that could go wrong and what they may think of you.

8. You get upset with yourself when you do something you feel was not right.

9. If you can't settle a difference of opinion with another, you try to avoid them altogether.

10. When you are criticized for your performance, you get upset.

If you answered "yes" to seven or more of these, this indicates that you suffer from excessive addiction to the need for acceptance.

If you answered "yes" to three or more of them, this generally indicates that you look down on yourself more often than you should.

If you answered "yes" to less than three of the questions,

you have a fairly healthy sense of self-worth.

When we begin to feel good about ourselves, others will also begin to feel good about us as well.

Let's look at some of the ways we use to gain acceptance from others.

Always competing, trying to be better than others.

Feeling guilty so that others feel sorry for you.

Being a martyr and letting others walk on you.

Trying to please by always rescuing others.

Always complaining trying to gain support.

Using excuses so that others think you're perfect.

Pretending so that we look good in the eyes of others.

Being a workaholic so that others notice your value.

Always giving advice so that others will think you know it all.

Justifying your position to keep from admitting that you are wrong.

Criticizing others so that others don't expect too much of you.

Flaunting money so people will notice you.

Being shy so that people give you more attention.

Always suffering so people give you more attention.

Losing so others will feel sorry for you and give you more attention.

Sacrificing so others will feel sorry for you and give you more attention.

Gossiping so others think that you've got the inside scoop.

Overtalking for attention, so that others will think you know it all.

Saying "I'll try" so that you appear to be able to help everyone, without commitment.

Let's look at a few of these in greater detail.

Saying "I'll Try"

Often this action can reflect both a need to control and a need to receive acceptance. Let's say that someone invites us to a party, and we say that we'll "try our best" to be there. By saying "I'll try," we didn't have to fully commit, just in case we couldn't make it. We say that we're going to "try" to attend the party, then we don't show. When asked why we didn't show, we simply say that we said that we would "try," but something else came up.

The next time you hear "I'll try" from another, stop and ask for either a yes or a no. If you are the one saying it, stop and give a yes or a no. This will avoid a lot of nonresourceful feelings in both the giver as well as the receiver and break the chain of pain.

Remember that our words carry power. They are hypnotic. They can empower or disempower. For example, to *try* means to struggle. So when we either say or accept an "I'll try," we are setting ourselves up for struggle. We say "I'll try," then we plunge into a nonresourceful state, trying to figure out an appropriate way to get out of the commitment that we didn't truly want to make in the first place.

The reason we put ourselves through all these gyrations is our need for acceptance. We are afraid of what the other person might think of us if we simply say, "No, I can't make it."

I was preparing to present a workshop in New York when I received a call from someone inquiring about the program. He was an independent distributor for the company to which I was to present the program. He explained that he was starting a new sales organization and wondered what I would suggest he do to get off to a fast start. I said, "What I would do if I were you is to attend the program along with five of your new salespeople." I asked if he could do that. His response went something like this: "Yes, I'll be there if I can. I'm going to really try. And if nothing comes up, I'll be there for sure."

I interrupted him and asked, "Wait a minute. Was that a 'yes' or a 'no'?" He went through the same answer as before. I stopped him once again and asked, "Was that a 'yes' or a 'no'?" With some difficulty, he finally gave me a doubtful "No," that he couldn't have five new people there. He then gave me a doubtful "Yes," that he himself would be there. He attended, and after the program he told me that he wished he had the courage to commit to having his new people there as well, but he was afraid of his ability to convince them to attend. He was more than willing to say "I'll try," but he was not willing to truly make a commitment or even say, "I'll discuss it with my people and get back with you tomorrow and let you know for sure."

Workaholism

Typically, workaholics are into control, or at least it appears that way on the surface. In reality, there's almost always an underlying need to be accepted.

I recall a woman in a workshop in Montreal who said she was a workaholic. She said she worked fifteen to sixteen hours a day, seven days a week. On the surface she seemed to have a very strong need to be in control. Working was her life. She had no time for family, a relationship, to take care of her health or to just relax. All she had time for, she said, was working and making money.

When we began to explore her situation on a deeper level, we discovered that her overwhelming need to be in control and her workaholism were due to an underlying need for acceptance from her father. The unusual thing was that her father had been dead for more than ten years, yet she was still seeking his acceptance. Her controlling behavior was so strong that she would have carried it with her for the rest of her life had she not discovered her underlying need for acceptance and let it go.

We've heard it said that opposites attract. We've also heard it said that like attracts like. You may find two people together who both need acceptance. On the other hand you may find two controlling personalities together. But neither of these types of relationships typically lasts for very long. Most of the time they never get together in the first place. In fact, they usually aren't even attracted to one another, unless it is purely a physical attraction or to have someone to argue with on occasion.

In most relationships we find one person needing acceptance and the other needing to be in control to be accepted. In an extreme case, the acceptance-oriented individual wants someone who will have control over them so that they can get more attention and then complain about their hardships and their pain. They typically have a martyr-type personality, feeling that the needs of others are more important than their own.

The control-oriented individual, on the other hand, attracts someone who needs acceptance. By doing so, they feel that they are more in control of their own life and others around them, and will therefore receive greater acceptance.

The more extreme the need one has will determine the degree of need of their partner, whom they have attracted. One becomes a mirror for the other, each giving the other the opportunity to see what it is they need to let go of in order to have more balance in the relationship.

In a healthy relationship, if we are observant, we learn from what we experience and what we observe in ourselves. By doing so, over time, we become more balanced.

There will always be some degree of opposite needs within even a healthy relationship. One partner may be a little more controlling, and as a result may be more organized. Their partner, on the other hand, is more acceptance-oriented and may not be as well organized. In other words, the two personalities together can make up a well-balanced relationship. It's when they become extreme opposites that the conflicts arise.

The following is an example of an extremely out-of-balance relationship, and what was done to remedy the situation very quickly.

Why Opposites Attract

A woman in her mid-forties attended one of my two-day workshops in San Francisco. As she was registering, I noticed that she had a black eye, and several marks on her throat and wrists. She also had a busted lip. It was very apparent that she had been severely beaten. Later that day, when we began to discuss the issues of the need for acceptance and control, and how it applied in relationships, she began to share the problems she was having. She said that she had been involved in a total of six relationships in her life, three of which were marriages, and the other three were men she lived with for several years each. She also shared that all six were all extremely abusive, which included the one with whom she was currently involved.

During a specific group exercise, she discovered that she had a very strong need for acceptance, that was brought on by a traumatic childhood experience. Her father had been physically abusive to both her and her mother. As she shared information about her current boyfriend, whom she had been with for a number of years, she discovered two things. One was that her boyfriend had a very strong need to be in control. The second thing she discovered was that the man was exactly like her father. By attracting this type of person, this gave her the perfect opportunity to work out the differences she was still harboring with her father. So, from that perspective, they made a perfect match, at least as long as she was hanging on to her need for acceptance from her father.

I worked with her for about fifteen minutes or so following the exercise. I began by asking her if she liked feeling that way, to which she answered reluctantly, "No." I worked with her for a moment until she could truthfully answer "No" without any hesitation. The next question was, "Do you want to let that feeling of always needing acceptance go once and for all?" And she answered, "Yes." The next question was, "Are you willing to let it go?" The answer was an immediate "Yes." The final question for her was "When?" which she could not answer. As I repeated the process several times looking for that definite "Yes," that commitment to let it go, I got a multitude of answers. The answers ranged from "Maybe" or "Not right now," to "Later today" and "Maybe tomorrow." After some time she finally said "Yes," she would let it go now! The whole class felt her release and gave her a standing ovation!

I explained to her that this process may or may not have released her entire feeling, and that she might have to spend some time working with it on her own. She immediately responded with, "No, I am finished with it. I feel free for the first time in my life, now that I no longer have any need for acceptance from anyone, especially my current boyfriend."

She had apparently cleared her need for acceptance. The only thing that she hadn't cleared was her boyfriend. I encouraged her not to attempt to figure out the potential outcome and to just let go of her need to control what might happen, or how she was going to get rid of him. I encouraged her to just give it a little time before taking any action.

The next morning upon arriving at class, she couldn't wait to share with the group what had happened. She explained again that she had been in this very abusive relationship for over two years. She had been trying to get rid of the man almost the whole time, but he had no interest in leaving. He had even threatened her life if she made any attempt to leave. His last threat was just the morning before. When she left for the workshop he said, "If you ever try to leave me, I will kill you!"

She went on to explain that when she went home the night before, she felt there was something different even before arriving. When she walked in, expecting to see him in front of the television with his beer, she found not only was he not in front of the television, but he had packed all his clothing and belongings and left! He left her a note saying, "I will never be back!"

As a result of her letting go of the need to be accepted by him, she had cut the chain of pain, and he felt the cut. He intuitively knew that he no longer had someone that he could control, so he was off to find a new victim. This left her open to discover a compatible person who complimented her new self-image.

A few weeks later she called to share with me that she had found the love of her life. I spoke with her more than two years later, and the two of them were married, living in a happy, well-balanced relationship.

Let Go Before the Conflict

Letting go in advance is also a concept worth applying. With this method that you can utilize every day, you avoid setting yourself up for new problems that you'll have to deal with at a later date.

Let's say you need to make a telephone call to someone to confront them about an uncomfortable issue. Think of a real situation that you might have or that you're currently experiencing. Notice how it makes you feel. We've all felt it . . . the fear, the need for the other person's acceptance. In this kind of situation, we basically have one of three options:

Option one is to not make the call so that we don't have to confront the issue, and maybe it will go away. Here's what will happen. By not making the call, we have now satisfied our need for acceptance and replaced it with our need to control. In other words, "I have decided to control my fear instead of making the call." But what we are really saying is, "I have decided to honor my fear and my need for acceptance instead of making the call and resolving the issue."

Option two is to hang on to our fear and our need for acceptance, make the call and hope for the best.

Option three is to let go of our need for acceptance—thereby not giving any energy to our fear—watch it go away, then make the call with no attachment to the outcome.

It's a choice. We can hang on, honor our fear, come from a nonresourceful place, push the other person's control button and hope for the best. Or we can let go of our fear, come from a resourceful, loving place, and move past or rise above our fear. By coming from the heart, we connect heart-to-heart, bypassing both the need for acceptance and the need to be in control. With this approach, we are never disappointed with the outcome and never attached to the results. We just create a vision of the outcome, let go of our fear and play with whoever shows up to play! We can also choose to honor our fear, and that's okay if that's what we choose to do. But it's really good to know who's making the decision, isn't it?

It's always a choice. It's always good to know who's in charge of making the decisions that control our lives. Just remember that hanging on to either of these two needs puts another link in the chain of pain.

Overtalking and Underlistening

Overtalking is another example of how we seek acceptance from others.

I remember a woman in a class in Los Angeles. Every time I asked a question of the group, she was always first with the answer. At every discussion, she dominated the conversation with her opinions and advice. If someone else got a chance to share, she always added to their response with her expert advice. She would talk, talk and talk, endlessly. She was disrupting the whole class with her continuous advice. In fact, during the break, several people made it a point to comment to me about how distracting and disruptive she was. I decided to resolve the problem in a resourceful way.

In the middle of her next interruption, I stopped her and said, "Would you mind if I asked you a question?" She said, "No, not at all." I knew that she would love the chance to answer a direct question so that she could give her opinion. I said, "Here's the question: do you know that you talk a lot?" "Yes," she said without hesitation, "people tell me that all the time." I said, "So you know that you talk a lot?" She said, "Yes." Then I asked her, "Do you feel that your desire to talk a lot comes from your need for acceptance or your need to be in control?" After some time, she discovered a need for acceptance that had been created by a repeated experience she had had as a child. With some work, she let go of her need for acceptance. She also let go of her need to talk so much in class.

Six months later I received a letter from her telling me how her life had changed after her letting-go process. She said that she now felt truly in control of her life for the first time. She explained that she had much more time to listen and think since she wasn't so busy talking all the time. She said that her sales business had grown for the first time in years, and that her relationship was also improving.

Overtalking is often the expression of our urge to think. But in our culture, those who seem to think rather than talk tend to be considered uncooperative or not very knowledgeable. This belief encourages talking and discourages listening or thinking. Talking too much is not usually motivated by our desire to discover the truth, but rather by our search for acceptance. We believe that acceptance is given to those who say something that *appears* to be the truth, to those who say something interesting, and to those who say something well, but not necessarily to those who speak the truth.

When we speak mostly out of our need for acceptance, we actually see less of true reality. As we seek to offer more clever words, the deeper our need for acceptance grows. As we begin to observe ourselves with these two needs and to notice how we truly are at the bottom of all our nonresourceful feelings, and as we begin to let them go, we'll notice two things:

1. We'll notice our nonresourceful feelings beginning to wither away from lack of attention.

2. We'll notice our resourceful feelings being enhanced, and our lives working better overall.

Remember, the more we feel the need for acceptance or control, the less of each we truly have. When we let go of our need for acceptance or control, only then do we have any level of control or acceptance in our lives.

Become More Self-Observant

Becoming more aware of the automatic behavior response of needing acceptance or control requires our close self-observation. The next time you feel nonresourceful feelings such as anger, fear, sadness or anxiety, or stuck in any way, take a minute, observe yourself feeling this way, then ask yourself, "Is this my need for acceptance or control?" You can rest assured it is one of the two. But if you can't decide which, don't grow upset over the issue. Just observe the feeling, let go and move on.

Here's a simple exercise that will be very helpful. Pick a day to become self-observant. Observe your every action that day. Just watch yourself as though you were observing someone else. Observe your every word, your tone of voice in conversation. Observe your gestures, your actions, your thoughts and your feelings. Observe your own beliefs. Don't let any part of you go unobserved, for just one day.

As you observe, ask yourself, "Why did I do that? What

was the root cause of that behavior? What was my motivation for doing that? Was I seeking acceptance or control?" You'll begin to discover that many of your daily actions have no real value except to allow you to gain approval or to feel more in control.

Through persistent self-observation and letting go, we begin to strip away our addictive programming and our need for support from others to feel good about ourselves. Only through self-observation will we truly know the appropriate action to take in any given situation. Only through self-observation can we know reality. Self-observation creates reality.

The real effect of this process will be progressive. First, you'll begin to catch yourself after the fact. In other words, you'll catch yourself after an upset. Don't beat yourself up for catching yourself in the act. Instead, celebrate your discovery. Stop for a moment and ask yourself, "Why did I do that?"

After some time and with more experience you'll begin to catch yourself in mid-action, and you'll say, "Why am I doing this?"

As you get better and better at self-observation, after you practice it for a while, you'll begin to catch yourself before you take action, and you'll say, "Do I really want to take this action?"

Remember that any time we attempt to cling to either side of a duality, such as needing acceptance or control, we are also clinging to its opposite. Clinging and pushing away become the same. We attempt to hang on to someone we love, and they leave us. We hang on to the need for acceptance so that we remain in control, and instead we lose both acceptance and control. We want to push something away from us, and we can't seem to get it out of our lives. We want only pleasant people in our lives, and all we seem to attract are arrogant people. Our need for acceptance and control has attracted both to us. When we begin to accept that life is simply life and that different types of people are just a part of life, sometimes we get the good and sometimes the bad. Only then can we truly be free.

8

Love Is Our
Natural State

Love has no opposite.
It's an energy
that travels so fast
that it's everywhere
at once.
Even in the
darkest moments
love is always present

We all have moments when everything we do seems to work. During these times, great insights occur. We feel abundant, happy and trusting. We are refreshingly stilled inside; our usual nagging chatter is quiet and our energy flow is profoundly open. In this state we are able to experience our true nature and the full beauty of our surroundings. We feel alive, balanced and purposeful. Then suddenly, without any notice at all, this vibrant state disappears as mysteriously as it came. Our soaring spirits and creative abilities seem to fall to sleep, as we drift back into our old identity. We begin to once again buy into the illusionary, self-created tensions of doubt, fear and scarcity that restrict us from being in the moment and living to our full potential.

Imagine for a moment how you would feel if your heart and mind were completely clear of all stressful, nonresourceful feelings, and you were in a place of overwhelming joy and creativity. Imagine that everywhere you went you were completely relaxed and nonjudgmental, and you were certain that the world was totally friendly.

Take a moment and recall yesterday. How would you have

felt if you had known that everyone you contacted was sending you love, and that you radiated a beam of love to others? And no matter what people said, or how they said it, you could recognize their love-meaning behind it or their need for your love? Think of how centered, joyful and confident you would have felt and how little you would have needed from the outside world.

Do you realize that absolutely nothing stands between us and this experience except our own self-created expectations of how we believe life should be?

The Silent Whispers

I remember a man who attended my leadership program in Toronto. When it was over, he remained seated while everyone else left the room. I noticed that he looked a bit confused, so I walked over and asked him how he had enjoyed the weekend. He complimented the program, but added that he was dealing with a very serious problem. I asked if I could help. After some time, he finally confided that he thought he had a split personality, and he wasn't sure what to do about it. He explained that he had been to dozens of seminars and workshops, and when each program was over, he always felt the same way. At the moment the program ended, he thought that he could accomplish anything! But he also knew that when he got home, or maybe the next day, his other personality would take over, those silent whispers inside his head would begin pulling him back into his other identity, and very soon he would be right back where he had started.

I spent some time with him, explaining that this feeling of duality was not unique to him, but that everyone experienced it to one degree or another. What he was really experiencing was his own belief system, created by his past experiences. His other personality was nothing more than the beliefs and feelings he had become so attached to. The silent whispers were nothing more than his old beliefs and feelings surfacing, needing to be released before he could truly move past them. The feelings that we all hang on to are what keep our beliefs intact. The duality that we all experience (and perceive as either constructive or destructive) is actually a battle that has been created by our own fears. The experience of a lack at some point in our past is meeting with an intense desire to avoid the lack in the future. Both the lack and the desire to avoid it are based in fears. Our fear supports the problem and suppresses the feeling of lack, allowing it to return even stronger at a later date. So we can see why getting pumped up or motivated at a seminar without really dealing with the feelings that support the limiting belief, is incomplete and short-lived.

Here's another way to look at it. Let's say that a cute stray puppy shows up at our back door looking hungry. What do we do? We feed it, don't we? Then what happens? Right, it comes back! And of course it keeps coming back as long as we continue feeding it. And pretty soon, it's no longer a cute little puppy, but it has turned into a huge Great Dane that eats a lot more food than we ever imagined. But now we have grown attached, and so we decide to keep it around anyway.

Many of our experiences start out as simple little programs, but then as we feed them, as we begin to pay more attention to them, as we suppress them more and more, they become stronger and stronger. Eventually these little programs run our lives.

As an example, let's say that as a child you were told repeatedly that your room was a mess, and that you were incapable of keeping yourself organized. You were told this over and over by people you admired and loved, so of course you believed them. Today, as an adult, you find that your room is still a mess, and in fact your whole life is disorganized. Or, you might take an opposite approach and as an adult you become a cleaning, organizing fanatic.

Our Programs Run Our Lives

We keep our old programs alive by feeding them. What do we feed them? We feed them the emotions that we refuse to let go. The emotion is simply the feeling, or trapped energy surfacing, offering us the perfect opportunity to let go and to grow. The more we become upset with ourselves for how we are, the stronger the programs become that are upsetting us. And before long, just like the stray dog, they grow up and take over our lives. They become a stubborn attachment to a one-sided point of view, formed by our own conditioned beliefs and perceptions of how we think life should be.

Over time, by identifying with our old beliefs and programming and with our sometimes desperate attempt to create a new and better life, we begin to lose sight of what we really are. We become ego-driven, or we develop a dual personality. The ego is nothing more than the sum total of all our past experiences or programming. As a result of living from our past, we begin to experience some of the following nonresourceful emotions:

- Anxiety
- Strategizing our next victory
- Inability to relax
- Disappointment with whatever results we produce
- The drive to always want more
- Feeling that no matter how much we have it's never enough
- Inability to enjoy peace of mind
- Perpetual conflict with others
- Believing that our possessions are who we are

These experiences produce unhappiness, stress, sadness, fear, anger and hopelessness. They are all derived from our ego-driven needs.

On the other hand, when we begin to let go of our nonresourceful emotions, we find ourselves:

- Never being disappointed with results
- Feeling that everything is unfolding perfectly
- Open to attracting solutions easily
- Open to opportunities
- Living without anxiety
- Sensitive to our surroundings
- Finding unexpected solutions to seemingly unsolvable problems
- Calm and in control in any situation
- Always openhearted
- Always at the right place at the right time

These experiences lead to feelings of confidence, inner calm, courage, balance, openness, happiness and joy. In short, we are living from a state of love.

I read somewhere and noted in my journal, "It's as though the mind has been split in two parts, one part staying in touch with love, and the other veering into the ego. The ego manufactures a kind of parallel universe where the unreal seems more real than reality itself. Love casts out the ego the way light casts out the darkness. Love is real, and anything that isn't love is unreal."

Most teachings tell us to analyze the darkness (the ego or past programs) in order to reach the light. But in reality, darkness is simply the absence of light. When we release the darkness (nonresourceful feelings), light appears automatically. There is no need to pursue light or to push away the darkness. All we really need to do is stop focusing our attention on the dark and simply let the light shine through. There is truly no need to analyze either.

It's essential to our own growth to become fully aware of the structure that we have built for ourselves, in order to truly understand this concept of duality and how we allow it to control our lives. Even though it is artificial and not our true nature, unless we understand it we will continue to live from a position of fear and inner conflict. Living this way makes us cling to all sorts of self-centered judgments, which can create a great deal of discomfort in those around us and ourselves.

Because of our fear of pain, we build up this false structure in order to protect ourselves. True freedom is having the courage to risk being vulnerable to life as it unfolds, by letting go of the structure and allowing ourselves to experience life as it arises, moment to moment. When we live our lives this way, we truly and fully experience who we are, without conflict or pain. When we begin to experience and to let go of our fears, only then can we truly find happiness.

The Universal Laws Are Always at Work

As we discussed earlier, there are really two universal laws at work here: the law of restriction and the law of expansion. When we come from our old programming, or the ego, the law of restriction is always at work. Just like a workaholic, the more we work, the more we feel the need to work, and at the same time the less we actually accomplish.

However, this law of restriction can be immediately defused by applying the law of expansion. The law of expansion works within our true nature. It works when we're in a state of resourcefulness, when we're connected to source, when we let go of the dark, when we let go of our need to be in control of every outcome.

In this state we find ourselves:

- Full of self-confidence
- Aware that our *I can't* feelings offer a perfect opportunity to let go
- Open to receiving
- In the resistance-free universal energy flow
- Calm, peaceful and in control without effort
- Living free of internal bodily turmoil
- Understanding

When we are operating within the law of restriction, on the other hand, we feel:

- Stuck. We basically remain immobilized until acted upon by an outside force—maybe a friend or someone who encourages us; we read a book, or find something that inspires us to move forward out of our stuckness.
- Active and excited. We spend all our energy. There's so

much activity we're exhausted by the end of the day, yet we feel as though we haven't accomplished a thing.

If we are not self-observant, it can be difficult to recognize whether we are applying the law of restriction or the law of expansion.

There's a story about Leonardo da Vinci. He wanted to paint a portrait of Jesus Christ. He searched and searched, and finally found a young, olive-skinned man who was the perfect model for Jesus.

Many years later he wanted to paint a portrait of Judas, the man who betrayed Jesus. Again he searched and searched for the ideal model. Finally he found a man evil-looking enough to fit the part. As he approached the man, he discovered that he was the very same man who had modeled for Jesus years earlier.

The moral to the story is this: "A rope in the darkness can be mistaken for a snake." But does that make the rope a snake? Of course not. It's not the darkness that's the real problem; it's the lack of light. Our lower self, or ego, seems to want to keep the light out by restricting our energy flow and keeping us stuck. The ego has a life of its own, and it survives on attention to the darkness. It survives within the law of restriction.

However, if we use the ego messages as a signal to let go, they become our greatest gift. The ego can be both our enemy and our ally, depending on how we perceive and utilize its messages. The ego is nothing to fear. In fact, it is fear.

It is nothing more or less than trapped energy patterns within the subconscious. These patterns can be released any time we choose. Our ego is like a gravitational force field that has been built up as a result of fearful thinking and feeling, and the subsequent suppression of the emotions resulting from those thoughts and feelings, which draw us away from our true nature, away from love. Like a computer virus, it can attack the core system, showing a dark, parallel universe where it appears that only pain and hardship exist. All we need to do is empty the trash!

The Ego Is Real Only Because We Make It So

One of the commonly asked questions about the function of the ego is, "If the ego isn't real, how come I have so much stress and pain in my life?" The ego is real, but only because we make it so. Stress and pain exist only because the ego exists. It's a mistaken, ego-driven belief (past programming) that we must push life. Pushing is what keeps us in a stressful state. Our ego convinces us to struggle and try to change our outside circumstances, which causes the real reason for our suffering to go undetected. The real cause of our suffering is identifying with the ego instead of our own true nature. In other words, the thing we are chasing is what's causing us to chase it. The simple truth is this: the painful experiences we endure are the effect of the trap, not the trap itself.

For example, if we feel fear, the fear is not the real problem. The real problem is that we identify with the fear. We hang on to it, believing that we are the fear. It's like hanging on to the tail of a wild buffalo and wondering why we are in so much pain. Having fear doesn't mean that we are the fear, any more than hanging on to the tail of a wild buffalo makes us a buffalo, or flying in an airplane makes us an airplane.

There is no stress in the moment. Stress, fear or any other form of nonresourceful feelings come from reliving past experiences in present time. The ego is always living in the past. The ego is the past. There is no ego influence in the moment unless we allow it.

The standard question at this point is, "What am I doing wrong?" There is nothing wrong. In fact, you are right on track. All the stresses and conflicts in your life are sure signs that change is taking place.

Here's what's really happening all the time. When you challenge your old beliefs and your nonsupportive programs, the ego goes on panic alert! While the new you is gaining momentum, the old you is regrouping to prepare for another attack! The new you says, "I want to be free." The old you then steps in and says, "Yeah, but what about security?"

The new you says, "I'm going to start a new business." The old you counters with, "But what about that time you failed so miserably? Do you want to experience that again?"

The ego will always engage in denial in order to protect its correctness. The ego wants us to believe that, as the ego,

"I know." As long as we believe this illusion, we have become trapped in a closed box where no light can enter.

You can know this for sure: Every situation, every conflict, every nonresourceful feeling and emotion we experience is our opportunity to let go and move past it. It's our opportunity to get out of the box, to let the light shine in, to experience more of the feeling of self-love and to be able to share more love with others.

The Gift of Fear

Every conflict we experience allows us to more fully discover who we really are. Our circumstances never need to change; it is our outlook toward our circumstances that need to change. Instead of looking at what we are supposed to learn from a situation, we can begin looking at the gift, and what we can discover. In fact, in my opinion our life is about self-discovery!

Dropping nonsupportive feelings and emotions that support our beliefs does not require a change at all, but more of a recognition. Change is set in motion automatically when the original belief is challenged. Remember how we challenge a belief? First, by recognizing through self-observation that the belief is outdated. Second, by letting go of the feeling and emotion that holds the belief in place. Once the energy of the feeling is released, the belief is weakened and can be changed.

Self-observation and letting go are always the entry points to changing a belief. We could spend literally years in therapy, but until we make a choice to do it differently, to challenge our old beliefs through self-observation and letting go, there will be no real progress, only temporary patchwork solutions.

A police officer who attended one of my workshops shared an experience from twelve years earlier. He had been involved in a shoot-out that left him wounded and several innocent people, including a small boy, dead. He had been on a leave of absence ever since. Twelve years of twice-a-week therapy sessions had brought him no results at all. He said that his therapy sessions helped only until he reached the elevator.

He explained that his therapist encouraged him to talk about the incident and to analyze his feelings over and over, "to get it out in the open."

He said that what he had received from the two-day class and a fifteen-minute letting-go session was truly profound. He said that not once during the twelve years of counseling had anyone ever told him that he had the capacity to observe his feelings and to let them go. Within a month, I received a letter from him saying that he was no longer in therapy and was going back to work.

Until we understand that our old programs and beliefs are not who we really are, we'll continue refusing to realize the games we play with ourselves.

The Roles We Play

I was sitting on the sofa with my four-year-old son William Landon one day. I asked him what he wanted to be when he grew up. He said quite seriously that he didn't want to grow up, that he liked the little-kid costume he was wearing. I asked him if he really wanted to stay a little kid all his life, or did he want to grow up someday like Dad. He said that when he was ready to grow up, he would just change his costume, but until then, he would just keep the costume he had. That about sums it up, doesn't it? We are all wearing our costumes of that which we think we are, and who we want others to think we are. Some are wearing the costume of the victim, others the costume of the successful businessperson or the struggling employee. Others may be wearing the always-broke or maybe the lonely-heart costume.

What we experience as real is simply a reflection of our own belief systems, a reflection of our outdated, self-created programs that keep us enslaved and separate from our own true nature. We all glimpse real life once in a while, but we still find it difficult to experience who we really are, moment to moment, without our costumes.

Remember that nothing outside of us is a threat to us in any way. The only real threat is our own internal whispers created by our own beliefs.

A False Sense of Security

A question I sometimes hear is, "How can something that feels so right be so destructive? It feels as though fear, worry, anger and other nonresourceful emotions are in my best interest. They all seem to protect me in some way." This is because our emotions fill us with a momentary but false sense of security.

For example, if I get angry with you, I feel that somehow my anger will protect me from being hurt by you. I'm using my anger to avoid the pain of not being in control or to get acceptance for being right.

It's also important to know that how we feel has nothing to do with right or wrong, so don't get down on yourself for how you are feeling. Our feelings are just trapped energy wanting to be released. Right and wrong are never the issue.

The real issue is this: Does the way we feel support our vision of the outcome we want to produce? Does it expand our energy and take us closer to our objective, or does it restrict our energy and lead us further away? Does it add to the quality of our lives? Does it make us happy and fill our lives with joy? These are all questions we should ask when our feelings aren't resourceful. If the answer is no, it's not resourceful, we should simply make a choice to stop doing it! We should let it go and move on.

All our nonresourceful feelings and emotions are always based upon past experiences. They have absolutely nothing to do with what is happening right here, right now, unless we let them. If we allow them in, then they become just as real as when they originally occurred. Even though these feelings may seem to have survival value, in reality they are literally killing us. In other words, we are choosing to die simply by not fully living in the present.

How much time do you spend in a resourceful state each day? To put it another way, how much do you die every day, simply by not being fully alive? Wouldn't it be sad to reach the end of your life and discover that you had lived only 10 to 20 percent of it?

Your Life Drama

As we have discussed, life is just a game, a self-created drama. We wrote into our life script each of the actors in our drama, including the leading role. All the players in every drama pretend to have power, and at the same time they are all looking to someone or something outside themselves to give them their power. However, most people don't really want power over others. What they want is simply to be in charge of their own lives, to break free of their own dramas, their pain.

Truly powerful people never seek power over others. Why would they need to? The more we pursue power, the more powerless we become.

By the law of attraction, who we are is what we attract. If

we are constantly seeking power, we'll attract people who will threaten our sense of control. If we chase life by constantly being driven to have more or to do more, we become the chase. If we fear not having enough, we'll continually attract circumstances that trigger our fear of not having enough. Our authentic power comes from letting go and living resistance-free, not pushing against.

Our actions should grow naturally out of living our true nature, out of living our vision, free from the influence of outdated beliefs and programming. To seek to do before we seek to know only reinforces the old programs that we are trying so desperately to eliminate.

Remember that you are not your drama. Your drama is not you. It is only trapped energy, like the trapped words on this page. You could choose to read them over and over again, or you could simply choose to turn the page. Don't take your story personally; it is not you.

Defeat, failure, hurt, pain and all the rest of the feelings we experience in our dramas are merely memories; they don't exist in real life. We should stop asking the part of us that created our problems to give us the correct solutions. Our old beliefs, our ego can become the fault-finder if we allow it, or it can provide us with a mirror that leads us to find new solutions to living our lives to the fullest. A simple rule is this: any time a voice inside your head speaks to you without love and compassion, you should never believe it. Better yet, you shouldn't even listen! Instead, you should feel the emotion when it arises, see it for what it is—which is just energy wanting to be released—embrace it, and then let it go and move on.

The Misconception About Love

Darkness is the absence of light, just as fear is the absence of love. When we turn on the light by letting go of nonlove feelings, all we have left is love.

We hold some misconceptions about love, however. The first is that it comes from outside us, and the second is that it is secured through relationships. If we narrow love down to these two things, we are cheating ourselves out of the endless possibilities that exist within the power of love. Love is always present.

The nonlove feelings that we all experience come from not being present with ourselves, from looking outside ourselves or into the future somewhere for our happiness.

Love is a word that many of us find difficult to comprehend. It is sometimes used to explain pleasure: "I love chocolate-chip cookies." Or to express an intention: "I'd love to have this or that." Or to measure how much we care for someone: "If you really loved me, you wouldn't treat me this way." Or in some of the songs we hear, to express an addiction: "I'm hooked on your love." Or to express pain: "Love hurts."

Being "in" love doesn't hurt us; being "in" anger hurts us. What we really get from being "in" love is joy. To be "in" love means to be deeply connected to source. And the depth of that connection becomes stronger as we let go of the fear, doubt, anger and blame that we allow to run our lives. Whether we're talking about a relationship with another person, with God or with ourselves, it's all the same. The love that we are searching for is always present; it's only been covered up by all our fears. Love is the spirit that lives within each of us. It is our own true nature. It's who we really are. It's our authentic power.

Many traditions and religious disciplines teach that getting in touch with the spirit aspect or our true nature is a long, drawn-out process that requires a great deal of discipline and special techniques. The fact is that it is simple and easy. The thing we should realize is that nothing is so intimately a part of us as our spirit, our true nature. It can't be lost. It can't be separated from us. It *is* us!

Many believe that we are imperfect and need to develop ourselves into perfection, when the opposite is really true. We are already perfect. All we have to do is to let go of our self-created imperfections, which then allows our true nature to shine through.

Love and happiness are our natural state, and for that reason we continually search for them. They are one and the same. We intuitively feel the pull toward our true nature of happiness. We recognize love and happiness because they vibrate within us. Living with this knowledge will bring complete fulfillment. However, this can only happen when we release the layers of fear and conflict that create resistance in the first place.

When we resist the natural flow by giving attention to our fears, we are really resisting our own self-love, our true nature. We are resisting the love that is always with us. Only when we let go of our fears can we live resistance-free.

Trying to earn love by acting or being a certain way will always end in failure, because once we stop behaving in these conditioned ways, we are still left with self-doubt, which is exactly where we started in the first place. In order to end the search for real love, we have to go beyond behavior and start looking inside. When we do, we'll discover our real self, the self who knows on a soul level that love is all there is and that "I am love."

We know the truth and we experience our true nature in some way at every level of growth and awareness. When we uncover the layers and reveal the ego for what it really is, we discover the most basic truth of all: that compassion, happiness, peace of mind and love are our natural state.

Before we can fully realize this fact, before we can be filled with love, we must first be emptied of all that is nonlove. In order to be reborn into a new way in any area of our lives, we must first die to the old ways.

One of the most basic fears we have about letting go is the fear of the emptiness we believe will be there when we do. But in reality, when we die to the old, a vacuum is created for the new. That empty space is instantly filled with love. Trying to chase love is like trying to vacuum the carpet with a full bag. When we surrender a false belief, the vacuum is then filled with love, and it happens without any effort whatsoever.

We seem to be constantly looking back into our past, hoping to find some kind of guidance that will provide us with more love in our future. When we stop viewing the future through the filters of the past, only then do we have freedom from our past and no anxiety for the future, because only then do we truly exist where everything—including love—happens, and that's in the present moment.

When we begin to see that every seemingly painful event is truly a gift designed to show us the power of love, our true nature will then unfold. Remember: "What you pursue will always elude you. What you become is what you'll attract." If you pursue love, it will always be out there somewhere, in the next relationship, job or outside event. When you become love through the process of letting go of nonlove, you then step into the universal broadcast of love. When you exist in love, you begin to discover it in everything you do. You will begin to transmit it in all you do—through your touch, your thoughts, your words, your eyes, your feelings, your handshake, your smile and your very presence.

With one act of real love you can cancel out thousands of acts of nonlove. When you give love in this way, you actually raise your own vibration and in turn attract more love into your life—tenfold in fact. In order to truly give love to another, you must first be open to receiving it, because how can you give something you have not yet received? Receiving comes first, then giving. As you receive and give to others, you also give to yourself in return. Isn't that wonderful?

And of course the reverse is also true: What you withhold from yourself, you withhold from others—and again from yourself, tenfold.

One day, out of the blue, my four-year-old, William Landon, asked, "Dad, do you know how much I love love?" And I answered, "No, I don't, Landon. How much do you love love?" He said, "I love it more than anything." So, intrigued with the dialogue, I asked, "What is love?" He said, "It's getting hugs and kisses from you and Mom, and my brothers, and also from Grandma and my Uncle Rick. I miss them a lot when I don't get to see them. I also miss getting hugs and kisses from Grandpa, and I miss giving them to him. But, some day I'll see him again in heaven with God. I also miss God, but some day I'll be with him again." He then looked at me very seriously and said, "Dad, when I die, I don't want to be put into a box in a hole in the ground, with one of those markers on top of my head. I want to go back to God. God's love is the love I like best, so I want to be with him again some day, okay?" What could I say?

Think of someone you could give love to today. By simply considering giving love to someone, you will automatically open yourself up to receive love, so that you can then give it. And when you give it, you receive it back tenfold. Isn't that great? And with no effort at all!

Here's the most important point of all. Love only operates in the present. And by living in the present, you send love into your future and you heal your past.

The present is the only place where miracles take place. Do you know why? Because only love produces miracles, and love only operates in the present. When we exist in love, our whole life becomes an endless stream of miracles.

Wherever You Are, Be There!

In the Bible there's a saying, "And time shall be no more." This statement simply means, "One day we will all live in the present." Only our ego speculates about what will happen tomorrow, or relives what happened yesterday.

Another of my favorite quotes from the Bible is, "Many are called, but few are chosen." In other words, "Few listen."

We spend a great deal of our time pondering two questions. The first is, "Will I get something out of this?" The second is, "Will this cause me pain?" We may seem to be calm, but under the surface these two questions are always lingering. In order to avoid the pain and find our happiness, we take the same old ego-centered habit patterns we've used all our lives and attempt to create a new framework from which to live. It's like putting on dry clothes over wet ones and expecting to get dry.

We continue this lifelong habit of running after something. We run around in our self-created circle-eight trying to find the beginning or the end. What do you think will help us to find happiness and avoid the pain of life? Position? Money? Would that do it? How about the perfect relationship? Is that it? Power? Would that be the key?

Each and every moment is complete and full just the way it is. Right now, what does your moment hold? Happiness, anxiety, pleasure, discouragement? Each moment is just as each moment is, and our real mission in life is to truly exist in that moment. Another way to say it is, "Wherever you are, be there!" When you are willing to just be there, exactly as you are, life is always okay. If things go right, that's okay. If things go wrong, that's okay, too.

We only think of the emotional upsets we experience as problems because of the pain they create, and we want to avoid the pain. But the pain we feel is the result of our expectations, which are created by remaining focused on the past and projecting it into the future.

When we replace our expectations with aspirations, we see things from a completely different point of view. With aspirations, we can have the courage to remain in the moment, remain in resourcefulness and accept the results that the moment brings. I'm not suggesting that we avoid taking action to improve our circumstances. I am saying that if we don't get the results we want, we should accept it in the moment and take action out of resourcefulness in the next moment to make the desired change, rather than bringing our disappointment with us.

This moment is all we have. By living with expectations, our mind wanders into the past and the future. When we live our lives with aspirations, we can gently return to the present moment, where the real action takes place.

Getting rid of this false ego structure that we have created is the key. Actually, we are not getting rid of it so much as just seeing through it. As we begin to see through our own egos and realize more of that which we really are, our ego begins to lose its hold on us.

You Are Not Your Drama

Our stories and dramas literally run the world. Everyone has a story, but the good news is that we are not our stories. One of the most common stories is "Never enough. This isn't it. . . . I want more." Before long, other people's stories become our story. But in reality there are only about six stories in the whole world! We just pass them around our circle-eights, like a relay team trying to win a race that can't be won. It's a race with no finish line! If we take our story personally, we'll get stuck in all the little things in life.

Just remember to let go. Your story is not you. Simply create your vision of how you want your life to be and then play with whoever shows up to play. Hold your vision true, embrace your true nature by remaining in the moment and let your nonsupportive programs wither away from lack of attention. In order to help the world, we must first help ourselves. Every action we take is always based on our desire for acceptance. Our need for acceptance from others always stems from our need for self-love. This deep-seated desire causes us to seek power, money, fame and a need for acceptance or control. Unfortunately, love cannot be obtained in these ways. Only by letting go of these needs, existing in love and sharing our love from that free place can we truly find love and happiness. In other words, if we want to help the world, we must first help ourselves. We cannot show others, unless we know the way.

About the Author

J im Britt, author of *Rings of Truth* is an internationally recognized leader in the field of human performance. He began his search for truth in 1968 and today is considered one of the leading experts in human behavior.

Through years of research and personal application, he offers a unique blend of ancient truths with modern, practical application, delivering a heart-touching and soul-stirring message of awakening, love and personal transformation.

Regardless of your background, education or experience, Jim Britt's message is guaranteed to move you. Whether you are a reader of one of Jim's books or a workshop participant, it will be an indescribable, thought-provoking, emotional journey, leading to self-discovery and personal change. His unique combination of personal style and message content affects everyone. He will ignite your imagination for becoming all you can be.

Jim has influenced over 1,000,000 people with his "breakthrough methods" and unique style of teaching. Jim's "letting go" processes provide specific tools designed to eliminate unwanted feelings, emotions and outdated beliefs that block our success and happiness.

Jim is more than aware of the personal challenges we all face in every area of our lives in making adaptive changes for a sustainable future. He offers hope for a brighter tomorrow and the tools to make it happen.

For More Information About
Jim Britt's Work

The *Rings of Truth* Retreat Workshop
The *Authentic Power* Three–Four Hour Seminar
The *Authentic Power* One- or Two-Day Workshop
The *Authentic Power* Certified Trainers Programs
Keynote Presentations
Custom Training Programs

To order other tapes, books and programs,
or to schedule Jim Britt as your featured speaker
please write or call:

P.O. Box 1743
Grass Valley, CA 95945-1743
1-888-546-2748
e-mail: *jimbritt@gv.net*

For a free on-line newsletter:
www.personalgrowthtips.com

Also from Jim Britt
Rings of Truth

A profound and moving tale of one man's journey to discover his true self.

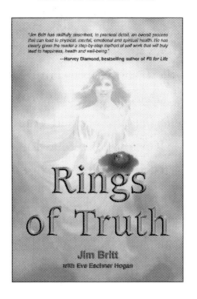

Code #7249 • Quality Paperback • $12.95

Matt a motivational speaker, has it all, until a spiritual apparition shows him that his material success means nothing if his soul is empty.

Join him on his transformative journey of awareness and awakening as he develops a greater understanding of who he is and teaches those around him, one truth at a time.